Edward J. O'Heron

YOUR LIFE STORY

Self-Discovery and Beyond

ST.
ANTHONY
MESSENGER
PRESS

CINCINNATI, OHIO

Nihil Obstat: Rev. Arthur Espelage, O.F.M.
Rev. Robert L. Hagedorn

Imprimi Potest: Rev. John Bok, O.F.M.
Provincial

Imprimatur: +James H. Garland, V.G.
Archdiocese of Cincinnati
May 19, 1992

Cover and book design by Julie Lonneman

ISBN 0-86716-177-9

Published by St. Anthony Messenger Press
Printed in the U.S.A.

Contents

Introduction

Flannery O'Connor once observed that most of the priests she knew were unimaginative. She need not have limited the statement to priests. Most of us lack imagination, or more precisely, we lack the use and the exercise of our imagination.

My purpose in this book is to address that lack. I invite you upon a journey to and beyond self-discovery through the use of your imagination.

A way to imagine yourself and your relationships with others is to use your imagination and your memory to look upon your life as a story (Chapters One and Two). Imagination and memory help you tell your story and listen to the stories of others (Chapters Three, Four and Five).

What follows in Chapters Six to Eight are exercises in imagination. They are ways of picturing yourself to yourself— specifically, picturing your past, your present and your future.

In Chapter Six you imagine your personal past through the image of climbing a mountain. In Chapter Seven you picture that point at which the future and past meet— known as the present moment— through the image of walking down a road. In Chapter Eight you imagine your personal future through the image of walking to the center of a circle.

Images and pictures help you understand yourself better. When you say, for example, "My life is a walk up a mountain," or "My life is a walk down a road," or "My life is a walk to the center of a circle," you are using these familiar word-pictures to shed light on something mysterious, namely, your life.

One of the intriguing aspects of an image or a picture in portraying your life is that it enables you to find more than one insight or come to more than one conclusion. A picture has more than one meaning. It offers you the opportunity to look at your life in new and different ways.

Poetry involves a making of connections or comparisons between what is known—in this case the word-pictures of climbing a mountain, walking down a road and walking to the center of a circle—and what is unknown, or at least in need of further understanding, namely, your life.

Up to and including Chapter Eight, your imagination focuses primarily upon yourself, what Martin Buber describes as the world of "I." In subsequent chapters your primary concern shifts "beyond self" to your relationships with others. Your primary concern at this point becomes what Buber describes as "thou," the world of "I and thou."

With the help of your imagination you enter the world of "I and thou" by picturing love relationships through images. In Chapter Nine you try to gain understanding from those images.

Like images, stories also contain more than one meaning. In Chapter Ten you turn to stories to shed light upon the mystery of human relationships.

Further light may be shed upon the world of "I and thou" by examining the subject of prayer. In Chapter Eleven special emphasis is given to prayer as a way we maintain contact with those we love.

The concluding chapter is an attempt to "stretch" your imagination. The chapter rests upon an unexpressed premise that we can begin to become what we imagine ourselves to be. An important step in imagining what we can be is to feed our imaginations with the stories of those whose lives illustrate some of the best of what a human being can be.

In Christian terms one image is the basis upon which all the other images rest. This image is not only an image but also a person—the person of Jesus, described by St. Paul as "...the image of the unseen God and the first-born of all creation,..." (Colossians 1:15).

St. Paul speaks of the Christian vocation as one of becoming more and more conformed to the image of God's Son, "We know that by turning everything to their good God co-operates with all those who love him, with all those that he has called according to his purpose. They are the ones he chose specially long ago and intended to become true images of his Son,..." (Romans 8:28-29).

There is a secret that has been kept too well for too long. The secret is that the Catholic tradition contains a wealth of riches that makes its appeal, first of all, to our imaginations. For many of us it is time to discover and recover some of that wealth.

Part I

The Story
of Self

Chapter One

Imagining Your Story

Imagination: What It Means

In George Bernard Shaw's play, *Saint Joan,* Joan is being questioned by a French officer. She says, "I hear voices telling me what to do. They come from God." The captain replies, "They come from your imagination." She replies, "Of course. That is how the messages of God come to us."[1]

This brief conversation illustrates two people using the same word, "imagination," in very different senses. The terms "imagine" and "imagination" tend to carry a negative meaning. If someone says, "You're imagining it," the general meaning conveyed is something like, "You're out of touch with the 'real world,' " or "You're seeing something that isn't there."

Works of imagination such as poems, plays and novels tend to be regarded at best as a change of pace from the important business of life and at worst as a distraction that keeps one from attending to what really matters. Imagination tends to be confined almost exclusively to the world of children in which story-telling, fairy tales and magic abound. It seems poorly qualified for a position in

[1] George Bernard Shaw, *Saint Joan* (Indianapolis, Ind.: Bobbs Merrill Co., 1975), pp. 68-69.

the marketplace of adult life.

Imagination is perhaps the most underrated and underused power of the human soul. Closely connected with the dismissal of imagination as relatively unimportant is a loss of a sense of surprise and wonder. Less and less do you tend to ask, "What is this reality in front of me?" More and more you tend to ask, "What is this for? What does it *do*? How can I turn it, twist it, manipulate it and make it something more valuable?"

The captain questioning Joan understands imagination in the popular sense of something unreal. By way of contrast Joan understands imagination in a more biblical sense as the human power through which "the messages of God come to us."

When we look at Jesus' style of preaching and teaching, we find that he appealed to his listeners' imaginations through stories and examples that they could easily picture for themselves. For example, he tells stories about a father who has two sons, a woman who loses some money she's hidden in her house, a rich man with a poor man at the gate of his house.

In addition to stories, he uses images such as a candle on a lamp stand, the birds of the air, the lilies of the field, the salt on the table. "The kingdom of heaven is like a mustard seed which a man took and sowed in his field. It is the smallest of all the seeds, but when it has grown it is the biggest shrub of all and becomes a tree so that the birds of the air come and shelter in its branches" (Matthew 13:31-32). He uses stories and images as a starting point for saying something about ourselves, our relationships with each other and our relationship with our God.

Let us try to set aside the negative meanings that have come to be associated with the term and look at the human power we call imagination. Imagination comes from the word "image," which means a picture. Imagination can be described as our capacity to create pictures in our minds, our capacity to create fantasies, our capacity to dream.

The Rational and the Imaginative

Our understanding of imagination is helped by research into left brain and right brain function. The left side is the rational side by which we analyze things and take them apart. The right side is the poetic and imaginative side.

In their book, *Whole-Brain Thinking*, Jacquelyn Wonder and Priscilla Donovan speak of left brain and right brain function, "The human brain's two halves have different but overlapping skills or ways of thinking:

Left		*Right*
Positive	Intuitive	Holistic
Analytical	Spontaneous	Playful
Linear	Emotional	Diffuse
Explicit	Nonverbal	Symbolic
Sequential	Visual	Physical."[2]
Verbal	Artistic	
Concrete		
Rational		
Active		
Goal-oriented		

Each person tends to prefer one side or the other. However, whichever side tends to be dominant, we still use both sides. Each of us is both rational and emotional, both

[2] J. Wonder and P. Donovan, *Whole Brain Thinking* (New York, N.Y.: William Morrow and Co., Inc., 1984), pp. 29-30.

goal-oriented and artistic.

Andrew Greeley uses the distinction of left-brain, right-brain activity and applies the distinction to religion in general and Christianity in particular,

> Religion occurs...in that dimension of ourselves that produces dreams, poems, stories, myths, and great or lesser works of art. Religion is a right-hemisphere activity, an altered state of consciousness before it becomes left-hemisphere behavior, before it becomes an ordinary state of consciousness. The poetic and imaginative dimensions of religion come before its propositional, cognitive, and theological dimensions. The Apostles had to experience the risen Jesus and tell their stories of that experience to others be- fore...theology, philosophy, catechisms, and creeds could appear. These later developments can and should not be dispensed with. They are essential because humans are reflecting as well as experiencing creatures, philosophers as well as poets, scientists as well as story-tellers.[3]

It is not a matter of choosing between the rational and the imaginative. However, there is a need to restore a balance between the two. Greeley notes in the history of American Catholicism an imbalance with the imaginative on the short end:

> Even a cursory study of the Catholic heritage will show that the form of Catholicism that has prevailed in this country for the last 200 years has stressed (though not without some vigorous dissent and criticism) the propositional and the disciplinary aspects of its heritage (as embodied in lists of doctrines, moral rules and canonical requirements) and has not emphasized enough the Church's experiential, imaginative, narrative, and communal dimensions.... [A] new set of emphases and concerns—

---

[3] Andrew H. Greeley and Mary Greeley Durkin, *How to Save the Catholic Church* (New York, N.Y.: Viking Penguin, Inc., 1984), pp. 24, 25.

is now required.[4]

George Bernard Shaw points out that some of the so-called "pure sciences" are not lacking in elements of imagination. He compares medieval doctors of divinity with modern physicists. The medieval theologians raised the question of how many angels could dance on the head of a pin. By contrast modern physicists raise and answer the questions about the dance of the electrons down to the billionth of a millimeter. Shaw draws a conclusion from this contrast,

> Not for worlds would I question the precise accuracy of these calculations or the existence of electrons (whatever they may be). But why those who believe in electrons should regard themselves as less credulous than those who believed in angels is not apparent to me.[5]

While we distinguish between left-brain and right-brain activities, between the rational and the imaginative, we do well not to try to separate them from each other. Indeed, each contains elements of the other.

The importance of imagination can be seen by examining its root word—"imago"—or "image" and the way that term is used when we speak of "self-image." Our self-image is the way we picture ourselves to ourselves. We speak of a good self-image or a poor self-image. We speak of the importance of a good self-image, which is another way of speaking of the importance of our imagination in picturing to ourselves who we are and what we are.

Some examples may illustrate the part that images play in our lives. You visualize yourself being looked at and gazed upon by someone, be it God or a human being. The

---

[4] Greeley and Greeley Durkin, p. xviii.
[5] Shaw, p. 48.

image of your being looked at tends to elicit feelings in you. If you examine the feeling, you may be able to name the feelings and gain insight into both the image and the feelings.

For example, if you imagine that the one looking at you loves you unconditionally, that is, with no conditions required before the love is given, the feelings evoked in you by that image will tend to be feelings of peace and contentment.

Suppose, by way of contrast, that you imagine that the one looking at you does not love you, that he or she does not wish you well and is watching you only for the purpose of waiting until you make your first mistake, in order to say, "Aha! Gotcha!" The feelings that tend to be evoked in you in this instance tend to be those of anger and resentment.

At first glance the image of being gazed at or looked upon by another appears to be a neutral image. Yet a closer examination reveals that the image tends to be surrounded by layers of feelings.

The connection between an image and feelings is explored by Bernard Lonergan. He distinguishes the image as image, the image as symbol and the image as sign.[6] To use one's national flag as an example, the image as image refers to the image's visible content, e.g., red and white stripes with white stars on a field of blue on the American flag.

The image as symbol is the image that is joined to feelings. Lonergan's definition of a symbol is "an image of a real or imaginary object that evokes a feeling or is evoked by a feeling."[7] As a symbol a national flag will tend to evoke

[6] Bernard J.F. Lonergan, S.J., *Insight* (New York, N.Y.: Harper and Row, Publishers, 1978), p. 533.
[7] Bernard J.F. Lonergan, S.J., *Method in Theology* (Minneapolis, Minn.: Winston Press, Inc., 1987), p. 64.

a wide range of feelings on the part of a nation's citizens as well as on the part of the citizens of nations friendly or hostile toward that nation.

A symbol, such as the national flag, may also evoke opposite feelings in the same person. Lonergan speaks of the capacity of a symbol to contain "the opposites." He says of a symbol, "It admits the *coincidentia oppositorum* [opposites], of love and hate, of courage and fear,...."[8] The flag will tend to evoke feelings of pride in you when you see your country acting in a humane way. It will tend to evoke feelings of distress in you when you see your country acting contrary to its humane ideals.

The image as a sign is the image to which a specific meaning has been given. Out of all the feelings that the symbol of the flag may evoke, out of all the possible meanings this symbol may have, when you say, for example, "Our national flag is a sign of human liberty," this many-sided image we call a symbol becomes a sign. In Lonergan's words, "As sign, the image is linked with some interpretation that offers to indicate the import of the image."[9]

To give to an image a specific meaning or interpretation does not prevent you from assigning other specific meanings to that image. You may say, for example, "Our flag is a sign of the struggle for human liberty not yet achieved" or "Our flag is a sign of 'being home.' " An image is capable of many meanings.

[8] Lonergan, *Method in Theology*, p. 66.
[9] Lonergan, *Insight*, p. 533.

Imagination: The Difference It Makes

What difference does the way we picture or imagine ourselves make? It can make quite a difference. If you imagine yourself letting go of undue anxieties and fears, you are more likely to begin to let go of undue anxieties and fears. If you picture your life as manageable, you are more likely to find your life manageable. In the words of William Lynch, "The greatest vocation of the imagination, as Martin Buber says, is to imagine reality, whether by finding or making it."[10]

The distinction between the use of your imagination to find reality or to make reality is easy enough to describe. If you use your imagination to visualize something that isn't there, you can say that you are making reality in the sense that you are creating something in your imagination that does not exist. By way of contrast if you use your imagination to visualize something that does exist, you can say that you are finding reality, in the sense of discovering what is already there, something which without your use of imagination you might not have found.

While the distinction between finding and making reality is clear enough in itself, in practice the difference is often less clear.

An example may illustrate. One way to visualize your life is to look upon yourself, your life, your talents and your relationships with others as a sacred fire that has been placed in your hands. A variation on this image is to imagine yourself surrounded by or enveloped in a flame.

Either way, you ask yourself: In this use of my imagination am I making reality or am I finding reality?

The immediate and more obvious response is that you

[10] William F. Lynch, S.J., *Christ and Prometheus: A New Image of the Secular* (Notre Dame, Ind.: University of Notre Dame Press, 1970), p. 64.

are making reality. The commonsense comment of an observer would be that there is no evidence of the existence of a flame in your hand or a flame surrounding you. Therefore, the observer would conclude that you are making something out of nothing and in that sense that you are making or creating a kind of reality for yourself.

That's the obvious interpretation of the visualizing you're doing. There is another, less obvious interpretation. In the words of Mike and Nancy Samuels,

> [P]hysicists have...begun to study subtle body ener-
> gies and their effects on the world outside the body....
> Kirlian photography, which studies high frequency
> electrical fields, has visually demonstrated that
> energy fields seem to surround objects and living
> things. The energy fields around people's fingers
> have been shown to vary with mood, and to be
> stronger around psychic healers while they are
> healing.[11]

Some physicists are now exploring energy fields, electrical fields and auras that surround humans. So when you visualize yourself surrounded with light or surrounded with a flame, you will agree with the "common sense" observer that in some way *you* are making reality. You will go on to say that through your use of imagination you are also finding reality in the sense of discovering something that is already there. Some physicists are now beginning to probe into a "reality" that your imagination has provided you with for a long time, namely, "I am a fire" and "I am afire."

Imagination can have an enormous influence upon your thoughts, feelings, behavior and existence. The importance of the way in which you imagine a situation you are facing is

---

[11] Mike and Nancy Samuels, *Seeing With the Mind's Eye* (New York, N.Y.: Random House, Inc., 1975), pp. 70, 269.

illustrated in Shakespeare's play, "Henry V." The king
speaks to two of his men prior to the battle of Agincourt,

> "Gloucester, 'tis true that we are in great danger;
> The greater therefore should our courage be.
> Good morrow, Brother Bedford, God Almighty!
> There is some soul of goodness in things evil,
> Would men observingly distill it out—
> For our bad neighbour makes us early stirrers,
> Which is both healthful and good husbandry.
> Besides, they are our outward consciences,
> And preachers to us all, admonishing
> That we should dress us fairly for our end.
> Thus may we gather honey from the weed
> And make a moral of the devil himself."[12]

The king is aware of the dangers facing all of them. Yet
he portrays the danger to himself and to his men as an
opportunity from which good can come. He sees that his
men will tend to think about, speak about and react to the
dangers according to the way in which they have pictured
those dangers to themselves. If they picture the dangers as
overwhelming them, they are more likely to be over-
whelmed by them. If they picture the dangers as difficult
but manageable, they are more likely to manage the
dangers and to draw good from them. The king assures
them that they can draw good from the present danger and
even "make a moral of the devil himself."

In his Letter to the Romans St. Paul speaks in a similar
way,

> Nothing therefore can come between us and the love
> of Christ,..... For I am certain of this: neither death nor
> life, no angel, no prince, nothing that exists, nothing
> still to come, not any power, or height or depth, nor
> any created thing, can ever come between us and the

[12] William Shakespeare, *The Complete Works of Shakespeare*, eds. I. Ribner
and G. L. Kittredge (Toronto: Ginn and Co., 1971), *Henry V*, IV, i, 1-12.
Further quotations from Shakespeare are from this edition.

love of God made visible in Christ Jesus Our Lord.
(Romans 8:35, 38-39)

He lists the dangers outside oneself and within oneself
which we may face; he pictures the dangers, any and all of
them, as incapable of standing between us and the love of
God. His invitation is to an inner assurance when and as we
face life's dangers, for what matters most is not the danger
we face but rather our response to the danger we face. In
turn our response will be influenced by the way we imagine
ourselves in relation to the danger we are facing.

Carl Jung gives an illustration of ways we can imagine
ourselves not only in relation to dangers but also in relation
to all of life's circumstances. He speaks of the process of
becoming the individual person one is called to become as
an ongoing lifetime process. He provides us with a picture
by saying that the failure or the success in becoming the
person we are called to be is like the difference between
being dragged through one's life and walking through
one's life upright.[13]

One of the ways to try to learn more about yourself is to
try to discover the images that are at work in your life,
especially those that touch upon the way you picture or
view yourself and your life. If you imagine yourself walking
through your life upright, you are more likely to walk
through your life upright, rather than being pushed, pulled
or dragged through either by circumstances or by other
people. You can begin to become and begin to be what you
imagine yourself to be.

[13] Carl G. Jung, *Answer to Job*, trans. R.F.C. Hull (New York, N.Y.: Meridian
Press, 1960), p. 185.

Questions for Reflection and Discussion

1) Are you a left brain or a right brain person? Give examples.

2) Using the left brain/right brain distinction, would you be helped by trying to develop the less preferred side? If so, how do you go about it?

3) Are Andrew Greeley and Mary Greeley Durkin correct in speaking of the Catholic Church in this country as too much left brain and not enough right brain? Give examples.

4) If groups of people as well as individuals may be described as left brain/right brain, how would you describe the society you live in? Why? Give examples.

5) Using Bernard Lonergan's description of a symbol as an image that evokes feelings, e.g., one's national flag, what are some of the personal images in your life that evoke feelings?

Exercise

 This is an exercise in the use of self-imagery. Find a quiet place where you will be alone and in silence. Relax. Be at ease. Choose an image and see yourself surrounded by and immersed in that image.

Three of the most common images to choose from are light, fire or water. If you choose light, imagine and visualize yourself immersed in light, radiating light. If you choose fire, see yourself fully enveloped in a flame that is both cooling and warming. If you choose water, see yourself surrounded with water, saturated as the waves break over you, around you, within you.

After a moment or two you may find yourself distracted by, for example, a problem you faced yesterday or a problem you're going to be facing tomorrow. During these moments you then surround the problem/persons/ situations that come to mind with light/fire/water. The distractions will cease to be distractions because they will be the "raw material" that you surround with light/fire/ water. Then let go of these distractions.

Choose a Scripture phrase related to the image you are using. For example, "Let there be lights..." (Genesis 1:14); "For our *God* is a *consuming fire*" (Hebrews 12:29); "...the water that I shall give will turn into a spring inside him, welling up to eternal life" (John 4:14). Slowly repeat the phrase.

When worries, anxieties and concerns continue to rise in your mind, continue to surround them with light/fire/ water. Thank God for the gift of light/fire/water. Let the image serve as a reminder that you are not alone.

Suggestions for Further Study, Reflection, Exploration

1) *Seeing With the Mind's Eye* by Mike Samuels and Nancy Samuels (New York: Random House, Inc., 1975) is a good introduction to understanding and exercising your imagination. Chapter titles include "A Brief History of Imagery in Religion, Healing and Psychology," "Medicine and Healing," "Creativity" and "Spiritual Life."

2) *Whole-Brain Thinking* by Jacquelyn Wonder and Priscilla Donovan (New York: William Morrow and Co., Inc., 1984) explains left brain and right brain function.

Chapters include "The Split-brain Theory," "Knowing Yourself Right or Left," "Getting the Feel of Right or Left."

3) *How to Save the Catholic Church* by Andrew M. Greeley and Mary Greeley Durkin (New York: Viking Penguin, Inc., 1984) explores the uses of imagination in relation to the Catholic Church. For example, they use and expand upon David Tracy's distinction (see below) between Catholic imagination and Protestant (and Islamic and Jewish) imagination.

The distinction is that Catholic imagination tends toward an emphasis upon the similarities between God and creation whereas Protestant, Jewish and Islamic imaginations tend toward an emphasis upon the differences between God and creation.

This distinguishing and describing of various religious imaginations is found in David Tracy's *The Analogical Imagination* (New York: Crossroad, 1981).

Chapter Two

Remembering Your Story

Memory: What It Means

In Evelyn Waugh's novel, *Brideshead Revisited*, the narrator Charles Ryder says, "My theme is memory, that winged host that soared about me one grey morning of war-time.

"These memories, which are my life—for we possess nothing certainly except the past—were always with me."[14] Ryder not only acknowledges the importance of memories but also equates them with his life.

However, remembering, like imagining, tends to have a negative meaning. Remembering tends to be equated with talking about a moment in the past known as "the good old days." It tends to be equated with "crying over spilled milk" or refusing to face the present or the future. It tends to be looked upon at best as an idle exercise and at worst as something that takes attention from the present and the future.

True, there are harmful kinds of remembering, as, for example, in the nursing of grudges or the seeking of revenge. To say that someone has a long memory is to speak, perhaps, in the context of a memory that serves

[14] Evelyn Waugh, *Brideshead Revisited* (Boston, Mass.: Little, Brown and Co., 1945), p. 225.

retaliation or revenge. In *Strange Interlude* Eugene O'Neill touches upon the human tendency to remember in a harmful way, "...[W]hat beastly incidents our memories insist on cherishing!...the ugly and disgusting...the beautiful things we have to keep diaries to remember!"[15]

Yet remembering, in and of itself, is much more than the sum total of its distortions and misuses. Memory has a variety of meanings. We say of someone that she has a good memory for facts or a good memory for remembering names. These are valid descriptions of the use of memory. They are examples of what Marcel Proust described as "the memories of the intellect."[16] Memory, as we shall speak of it here, however, involves more than remembering names, facts and faces. We speak of memory here in a deeper, more personal sense that goes to the heart of our dignity as persons, what we may describe as the memories of the heart.

For example, when Charles Ryder speaks of the memories that are his life, we may assume that he means something more than the memories of the intellect. We may assume that he is speaking of the memories that engage his entire person—body and soul, mind and heart. Only those memories that in some way are linked with what is deepest within himself does he equate with his "life."

In his *Confessions* St. Augustine gives considerable attention to the subjects of time and memory. He recasts the traditional distinction of past, present and future,

> It is not properly stated that there are three times: past, present and future. But perhaps it might properly be said that there are three times, the

[15] Eugene O'Neill, *Strange Interlude* (New York, N.Y.: Random House, Inc., 1959), p. 79.
[16] Marcel Proust, *Remembrance of Things Past* (New York, N.Y.: Random House, Inc., 1981), Volume I, p. 47.

present of things past, the present of things present
and the present of things future.[17]

What Augustine refers to as the present of things past is
the dominant theme as well as the title of Marcel Proust's
The Remembrance of Things Past. Proust makes a distinction between the place that human beings occupy in space
and the place they occupy in time,

> But, at least, if strength were granted me for long
> enough to accomplish my work, I should not fail...to
> describe men first and foremost as occupying a place,
> a very considerable place, compared with the
> restricted one which is allotted them in space, a place
> on the contrary prolonged past measure...in the
> dimension of time.[18]

While the place you occupy in space is a very limited
one, the place you occupy in time is an exalted place
because through your memory you have immediate access
to past moments that have occurred in the story of your life.
You are not "hemmed in" only to the present moment in
time as you are "hemmed in" to the physical place you
currently occupy.

Moreover, it is only with a proper relationship with our
past that we can hope to understand ourselves and create
our future. As Simone Weil says, "We possess no other
life...than the treasures stored up from the past and
digested, assimilated and created afresh by us."[19]

Carl Jung speaks in similar fashion, "[I]t is precisely the
loss of connection with the past, our uprootedness, which
has given rise to the 'discontents' of civilization.... The less
we understand of what our fathers and forefathers sought,

---

[17] Augustine, *The Confessions of St. Augustine*, trans. John K. Ryan (Garden
City, N.Y.: Doubleday and Co., Inc., 1960), p. 293.
[18] Proust, Vol. III, p. 1107.
[19] Simone Weil, *The Need for Roots* (Boston, Mass.: Beacon Press, 1952),
p. 8.

the less we understand ourselves....[20]

Indeed, as Jung continues, "[W]henever we give up, leave behind, and forget too much, there is always the danger that the things we have neglected will return with added force." [21]

Memory and Scripture

The connection between memory and what is deepest within ourselves is a refrain often found in the pages of Scripture. When we turn to the Old and New Testaments, we find that much of what we are called to can be summed up in a single word—remember. Remember who you are. Remember what you are called to: "...I have told you all this, so that...you may remember that I told you" (John 16:4).

Remember the Lord God who has called you: "Remember how Yahweh your God led you for forty years in the wilderness, to humble you, to test you and know your inmost heart—whether you keep his commandments or not" (Deuteronomy 8:2). Remember what he has done and is doing for you: "remember the marvels he has done, his wonders, the judgements from his mouth" (1 Chronicles 16:12).

Remember the people who have made and are making a difference in your life: "I thank my God whenever I think of you...remembering how you have helped to spread the Good News from the day you first heard it right up to the present" (Philippians 1:3-5). This kind of remembering is more than a photographic recollection of names, dates and

---

[20] Carl G. Jung, *Memories, Dreams, Reflections* (New York, N.Y.: Random House, Inc., 1963), p. 236.
[21] Jung, p. 277.

places, although it may include these.

Two Kinds of Time

Memory brings us images from another time. Actually, there are two kinds of time as expressed by the Greek words, chronos and kairos. Chronos is chronological time as we know it, minute by minute, hour by hour. Kairos is the special moment, the transforming moment that's not to be measured merely with clock and calendar.

Of the special moment John McKenzie notes, "The Hebrew and Greek words which are translated 'time' indicate a point of time; and the point is identified by the event which is associated with it."[22]

The Sinai event is kairos, a sacred moment, what Rosemary Haughton describes as a "breakthrough" event. Sacred moments, like God's revelation to Moses on Mount Sinai, can be better seen in the light of this biblical understanding of time.

Sacred moments may be described as special moments and special opportunities which give a new meaning or a new direction to one's life. These sacred moments may be described in various ways as "turning points," "moments of truth," "peak experiences," "crisis," "change," "being born again," "conversion." Rosemary Haughton cites some examples,

> This can be a small personal event, such as the achievement of a shared understanding. It can be a physical event, such as the breaking of a dam, where the 'need' of the water to find a way forward breaks the barriers and crashes through to the valley below. It can be a mystical experience or a scientific

[22] John L. McKenzie, *Dictionary of the Bible* (New York, N.Y.: Macmillan Co., Inc., 1965), p. 891.

discovery. It can be a chicken breaking its shell or the signing of a peace treaty.[23]

Andrew Greeley indicates that sacred moments in people's lives may be far more frequent than they are assumed to be.[24] He cites examples of surveys which indicate that a majority of the people surveyed said that they have undergone some form of deep, transforming religious experience in their lives. At the same time many of the people involved have said nothing about their experiences to anyone lest they be dismissed as "abnormal" or "crazy."

One example of sacred moments in one's life goes by the name of conversion. Conversion literally means "turn" which can be understood as a turning from and a turning toward. The term "convert" often refers to one who has become a member of a particular religious faith group.

In accord with the biblical injunction, "You will be able to tell them by their fruits" (Matthew 7:16), Bernard Lonergan speaks of that change of direction that conversion implies. He describes some of the signs of genuine conversion. He focuses not so much upon the experience itself but rather the aftereffects resulting from the experience:

> Conversion is a change of direction and, indeed, a change for the better. One frees oneself from the inauthentic. Harmful, dangerous, misleading satisfactions are dropped. Fears of discomfort, pain, privation have less power to deflect one from one's course. Values are apprehended where before they were overlooked. Scales of preference shift. Errors, rationalizations, ideologies fall and shatter to leave

[23] Rosemary Haughton, *The Passionate God* (Mahwah, N.J.: Paulist Press, 1981), p. 18.
[24] Andrew Greeley discusses this subject at length in *Ecstasy: A Way of Knowing* (Englewood Cliffs, N.J.: Prentice-Hall, Inc., 1974).

one open to things as they are and to man as he
should be.[25]

In a wider sense conversion means a turning from the
surface of one's life and a turning toward the depth of one's
life. Paul Tillich places conversion in this wider sense into a
religious context by indicating that another name for God is
"the Depth" of one's life:

> The name of this depth and ground of all being is
> God. That depth is what the word God means. If the
> word God does not have much meaning for us, let us
> translate it and speak of the depth of our life, of our
> ultimate concern, of what we take seriously without
> any reservation.[26]

Another example of sacred moments is found in the
experience of those who have had "close calls" with death.
In *Life After Life* Raymond Moody describes a typical
experience. What is said of the "close call with death"
experience can also be said of most sacred moments:

> Later he tries to tell others, but he has trouble doing
> so. In the first place, he can find no human words
> adequate to describe these unearthly episodes. He
> also finds that others scoff, so he stops telling other
> people. Still the experience affects his life
> profoundly....[27]

Relationship of Past Moments to the Present Moment

Now your attention focuses not so much upon the
sacred moment but rather upon the remembering of the

[25] Lonergan, *Method in Theology*, pp. 176, 177.
[26] Paul Tillich, *The New Being* (New York, N.Y.: Charles Scribner's Sons,
1955), quoted in *I'm O.K., You're O.K.* by Thomas Harris (New York, N.Y.:
Harper and Row Publishers, Inc., 1967), p. 233.
[27] Raymond Moody, *Life After Life* (Covington, Ga.: Bantam/Mockingbird
Books, 1976), pp. 22-23.

sacred moment, not so much upon the event or experience as such but upon your recapturing and treasuring it through memory.

Through your remembering of a past moment, a wedding of the past moment and the present moment can take place. Marcel Proust says you "are plunged simultaneously in the past and in the reality of the present."[28]

There is a uniqueness in the sacred moments in your life, your awareness that they are an unmerited gift, your awareness that the best of human willpower, unaided, could not merit them. You are able through memory and imagination to recapture those moments of the past at the present moment. You can make the past moment present to you again.

You find this to be one purpose of a "quiet time" each day. A quiet time enables you to move beneath the often noisy and superficial surface of the present moment to recapture a past moment. One irony here is that in recapturing a sacred moment from the past, you are thereby transforming the present moment into a sacred moment as well. You are stepping outside time, enabling you to return to the present moment and to the order of hour-by-hour time enriched as a result.

The remembering of sacred moments can illumine your present moment and your present situation. This is the positive side of Santayana's comment that those who refuse to learn from history are condemned to repeat it. What is true of history in general is also true of your personal history. One need not repeat all of the mistakes of the past; your past moments can shed light upon the present moment.

[28] Proust, Vol. III, p. 544.

Proust compares the experience of recapturing a sacred moment from one's personal past to the experience of a resurrection:

> A minute freed from the order of time has recreated in us, to feel it, the man freed from the order of time. And one can understand that this man should have confidence in his joy...one can understand that the word 'death' should have no meaning for him; situated outside time, why should he fear the future?[29]

In the recapturing of a personal, sacred moment through memory Proust comes to the awareness not only that death is not the final word but also that physical death is not to be feared in the light of these "timeless" moments. This kind of remembering involves more than the recollection of a past moment. Both memory and imagination play a part on what amounts to, in some way, not just remembering but also reliving that past moment.

Up to now we have looked upon the union between a past moment and the present moment through the memory of a personal, sacred moment. There is, however, another way to look upon this union: the present moment that illumines and enriches the past moment. Forgiveness, a special exercise of memory, is a good example.

The "raw material" of forgiveness consists of personal memories that may be filled with anger, guilt, resentment or a combination of all of these. Forgiveness does not mean that we try to deny the memory or to pretend that it does not exist. Rather, forgiveness presupposes our present awareness of what has happened, as expressed in the words of Lady Macbeth, "What's done cannot be undone."[30] The human action of forgiveness goes beyond that

[29] Proust, Vol. III, p. 906.
[30] Shakespeare, *Macbeth*, V, i, 65.

awareness by transforming the memory that needs to be healed.

In other words, if you hold a grudge, you are "stuck in your past." The phrase itself—holding grudges—indicates you are holding on to something you need to let go. Hugh Prather notes that the basic meaning of the verb "to forgive" is "to let go, to give up, to cease to harbor."[31] Nowhere does Jesus reveal himself more as a master psychologist than when he speaks about forgiveness. "[G]rant pardon, and you will be pardoned" (Luke 6:37). Now psychology comes along and tells us the same thing—that we achieve inner health through forgiveness, the forgiveness of others as well as the forgiveness of ourselves.

Without forgiveness there tends to be resentment or guilt. Instead of human connections, there tend to be separate prisons. Forgiveness is a decision.

After World War II when a Nazi concentration camp was liberated, a prayer written by a Jewish prisoner was found:

> Peace be to all people of bad will and an end to all revenge.... O God, to all the evil ones grant the benefit of the courage and fortitude shown by those others who were their victims.... Grant the benefit of the love and sacrifice of those suffering hearts, steadfast in the face of death.... May peace come once more upon the earth, peace to people of goodwill and peace to the others as well. Amen.

Forgiveness frees the forgiver, as well as the person who accepts forgiveness, prior to any response or lack of response on the part of those to be forgiven.

Some prayers are so familiar to us that we easily overlook what we are saying. In saying the Lord's Prayer

---

[31] Hugh Prather, *Notes on How to Live in the World...and Still Be Happy* (Garden City, N.Y.: Doubleday & Co., Inc., 1986), p. 24.

we are in effect putting ourselves on the line regarding forgiveness. We ask that we be forgiven in the measure with which we forgive others, "[a]nd forgive us our debts, as we have forgiven those who are in debt to us" (Matthew 6:12). As Jesus says on another occasion, "...the amount you measure out is the amount you will be given back" (Luke 6:38).

Through forgiveness a union between the present moment and a painful moment from the past is achieved. Through forgiveness the present moment transforms the bitterness, resentment or guilt connected with a past moment. It is not the painful moment from the past that is changed. Rather your relationship with the past, painful moment is changed.

In *The Merchant of Venice* Portia provides a reminder of the need for forgiveness:

> Therefore...
> Though justice be thy plea, consider this:
> That in the course of justice none of us
> Should see salvation.[32]

Justice is important and necessary. Without it we might not recognize the need for forgiveness. However, it is forgiveness—the willingness to forgive and the willingness to be forgiven—that makes the difference. Forgiving may be as close as we shall come in this world to fulfilling Jesus' command, "love one another, as I have loved you" (John 15:12).

---

[32] Shakespeare, The *Merchant of Venice*, IV, i, 194-197.

Memory and Prayer

One aspect of prayer easily overlooked is the relationship between prayer and memory. Whether alone or with others, times of prayer are times to let ourselves remember. Times of prayer remind us that often more important than what has happened to us is the way we remember what has happened to us. Often more important than the events of our personal past is the way we remember the events of our personal past.

Times of prayer give us a way of seeing, a point of view that enables us to see a love at work in the story of our lives, the love we call God. Times of prayer enable us to bring healing to some of those memories of ours that may be in need of healing.

Times of prayer remind us that one way of describing our personal vocation in life is that each of us is called to be a creator of memories for the people in our life.

Through the prophet Isaiah God says, "Does a woman forget her baby at the breast, or fail to cherish the son of her womb? Yet even if these forget, I will never forget you" (Isaiah 49:15). These words remind us of our God who remembers his promises, is faithful and does not forget his own. Each one of us is "his own," called upon to remember and to be grateful.

Questions for Reflection and Discussion

1) By way of linking imagination and memory, what images or pictures can you think of that are joined to some of your personal memories?

2) What are some examples to illustrate Jung's contention

that when we forget too much, there's a danger that what we've ignored will return with greater force?

3) Do you find that the special moments in your life resonate with Bernard Lonergan's description of the aftereffects of special moments?

4) From your experience of special moments can you add to Bernard Lonergan's list of the aftereffects of special moments?

5) What are some examples from your experience in which your remembering of a special past moment helped you at the present moment?

6) What are some examples from your experience in which the present moment has changed a past moment through forgiveness?

7) What do you make of the remark, "I'll forgive but I'll never forget"?

8) Is it proper to speak in any sense of forgiving God?

9) What are some examples of your memories that have been healed/are in need of healing?

Exercise

This exercise involves the use of your memory and your imagination in which a past moment transforms the present moment.

An example will help you practice using past moments to change the present moment. The story of Jesus' meeting with the tax collector, Zacchaeus, is described in Luke 19:1-10. Zacchaeus climbs a sycamore tree to get a better look at Jesus. Jesus greets him and accepts his hospitality. This moment became for Zacchaeus a conversion experience.

You can imagine that for Zacchaeus the image or picture of a sycamore tree became for him a doorway that reopened his past experience of meeting Jesus. In a quiet moment all he has to do is to visualize himself sitting in a sycamore tree or, as a variation, simply to visualize a sycamore tree and his past experience becomes present to him now.

To hold the image in his mind's eye leads him into a reliving of the past experience. The image is no longer just an image. It is now an image linked with his memory, his feelings and his lived experience.

For Zacchaeus for the rest of his life a sycamore tree will no longer be just a sycamore tree. From now on a sycamore tree, actually seen or visualized, will be connected with the life changing moment he experienced.

You can do the same thing. Choose a special moment or a special time from your personal past. Bring to mind a mental image or picture which for you is connected with your memory of the special moment.

Keep that image, your personal equivalent of Zacchaeus' sycamore tree, before you in your mind's eye. Let the image or picture lead you into your memory of that special moment. You are feeling now what you felt then. Let the past experience surround you. There is no need to try to analyze what's happening. Just let it be. Just let it happen.

Your reflective moment becomes a prayerful moment as you say "Thank you" while reliving the past moment. You are now moving into the two-step rhythm of remembering and being grateful.

"Thank you for this precious past moment. Thank you for precious past moments whose light continues to radiate upon present moments. Thank you for precious past moments whose light will radiate upon future moments."

Suggestions for Further Study, Reflection and Exploration

1) In *Gift From the* Sea (New York: Random House, Inc., 1965) Anne Morrow Lindbergh uses a vacation to the seashore as a setting for personal reflections. She uses various seashells as symbols of the life she has led and is remembering, her life at the present moment and the life she is contemplating for the future.

2) Autobiographies can be described as exercises in memory as the authors pick and choose from their personal pasts. In recent years Carl Jung's writings have drawn the attention of many who are interested in religion. Much of Jung's writing is not easy reading. However, his autobiography, *Memories, Dreams, Reflections* (New York: Random House, Inc., 1965) is quite readable and serves as a good starting point for those who wish to become better acquainted with Jung.

3) Simone Weil's *The Need for Roots* (Boston: Beacon Press, 1952) is divided into three parts. In the first, entitled "The Needs of the Soul," she speaks both of her personal past and the collective human past in relation to the soul's needs of which she considers the need for roots to be the most important as well as the least recognized.

   In the second part, "Uprootedness," she turns her attention to what is happening around her, namely,

France in the 1930's and 1940's. In part three, "The Growing of Roots," she makes connections between roots and the future.

Chapter Three

Telling Your Story

Your Life Is a Mystery

Your life is a mystery not in the sense that you can know nothing about it. It is a mystery in the sense that no matter how much you know and understand it, there will always be more to know and understand.

Mystery does not end with yourself. Other people are a mystery to you. This does not mean you cannot be in relationship with them nor understand them to some extent. Knowing them and understanding them does not do away with mystery. It opens up new areas of mystery.

The world you live in is also a mystery. As Carl Jung expresses it, "The unexpected and the incredible belong in this world. Only then is life whole. For me the world has from the beginning been infinite and ungraspable."[33]

Mystery in your life, the lives of others and the world around you is not a problem to be solved. A sense of mystery enhances your life. It gives you the opportunity to begin an adventure of discovery. To preserve a sense of mystery is to be a learner and listener. To preserve a sense of mystery means to preserve a sense of wonder and surprise.

[33] Jung, *Memories, Dreams, Reflections*, p. 356.

Telling Your Story

One of the ways you respond to the mystery of yourself, other human beings and the world around you is to tell your story and listen to the stories of others. Story in this sense refers not to fiction or a fairy tale but rather a true story as, for example, when you speak of "the story of my life."

John Dunne invites you to put your story into words and see "the elements of drama in it: the plot, the characters, the thought content, the modes of expression, the setting."[34] In the words of Shakespeare,

> "All the world's a stage
> And all the men and women merely players.
> They have their exits and their entrances,
> And one man in his time plays many parts."[35]

Your story can be told in many different ways. You have levels of depth within you. For example, telling the things you did yesterday in fulfilling your job description means telling your story at one level. Telling the story of how you felt or what you were feeling yesterday is to tell your story at a deeper level. The level is deeper because you are adding to the story a new dimension known as feelings, telling what you're experiencing.

At a still deeper level the telling of your story may involve some description of your personal state of being, such as, "Am I living 'in a state of inner assurance, a state of doubt, a state of quiet desperation'[36] or a combination of these internal states?"

---

[34] John S. Dunne, *A Search for God in Time and Memory* (Toronto: Macmillan Co., 1967), p. vii.

[35] Shakespeare, *As You Like It*, II, vii, 139-142.

[36] Dunne, *A Search for God in Time and Memory*, p. viii. Dunne also cites "Luther who compares hell, purgatory and heaven to despair, uncertainty and assurance," p. x.

Bernard Lonergan speaks of these various levels of depth within each of us, as revealed in our responses to other persons, "[O]ne is aloof with strangers,...occasionally unbosoms oneself to intimates, keeps some matters entirely to oneself, and refuses even to face others."[37]

Lonergan's words remind you that you do not tell your story in a vacuum. You choose with care when, how and to whom you tell your story. The deeper the level from which the telling of your story proceeds, the greater is the care and caution you use. Telling your story at one of its depth-levels requires and presumes an atmosphere of trust.

The possible distortions in telling your story are many. Your motive may be little else than an ego trip for the purpose of impressing others. You may consciously add or subtract from your story in ways that will make it flattering to yourself and critical of others. Yet all the possible distortions do not change the fact of the importance of telling your story.

When you tell your story to one who listens in a caring way or when you listen in a caring way to one who tells his story, something happens. George Eliot expresses the experience of what that something is or is like:

> Oh, the comfort, the inexpressible comfort, of feeling safe with a person, having neither to weigh thoughts nor measure words, but to pour them all out as they are, chaff and grain together, knowing that a faithful hand will take and sift them, keep what is worth keeping, and then with a breath of kindness blow the rest away.[38]

Looking upon your life and the lives of others as a story can help you find and give meaning to what is happening

[37] Lonergan, *Insight*, p. 470.
[38] George Eliot, *Middlemarch* in *The Works of George Eliot* (New York, N.Y.: Nathaniel Moore, 1908), VI, p. 287.

within and around you. As John Shea said, "We turn our pain into narrative so we can bear it; we turn our ecstasy into narrative so we can prolong it."[39] In Isak Dinesen's words, "any sorrow can be borne if a story can be told about it."[40]

You can look upon yourself and your story as both the starting point and the final destination referred to by T.S. Eliot, "We shall not cease from exploration/ And the end of all our exploring/ Will be to arrive where we started/ And know the place for the first time."[41]

Holy Mystery

There is yet another mystery beyond the mystery of oneself, other human beings and the world we inhabit. It is the mystery that is the source of all other mysteries. It is what Karl Rahner speaks of as "Holy Mystery."

Bernard Lonergan notes that there exists within each of us, "a region of the divine, a shrine for ultimate holiness. It cannot be ignored. The atheist may pronounce it empty. The agnostic may urge that he finds his investigation has been inconclusive. The contemporary humanist will refuse to let the question arise. But their negations presuppose the spark..., our native orientation to the divine."[42]

The awareness of Holy Mystery is a realization that all of our human experience and activity is sustained by this same Holy Mystery. To believe you are a living mystery is a starting point and a stepping stone to believe that your life

---

[39] John Shea, *Stories of God: An Unauthorized Biography* (Chicago, Ill.: Thomas More Press, 1978), p. 8.

[40] Isak Dinesen (quoted by Shea, p. 47).

[41] T.S. Eliot, "Little Gidding," *The Complete Poems and Plays* (New York, N.Y.: Harcourt, Brace and World, Inc., 1962), p. 145.

[42] Lonergan, *Method in Theology*, p. 103.

is joined to a Someone who loved you into life and loves your every moment of life though you have not yet met face to face.

> The most beautiful thing we can experience is the mysterious. It is the source of all true art and science. He to whom this emotion is a stranger, who can no longer pause in wonder and stand wrapped in awe is as good as dead.... To know that what is impenetrable to us really exists, manifesting itself as a wisdom and beauty which our dull faculties can comprehend only in their most primitive form, this knowledge and this feeling is at the heart of true religion.[43]

Edward Braxton speaks of a next step in which Holy Mystery is given a name. Holy Mystery is seen to be Someone we call God. Naming God includes not only such names as the "I Am" (Exodus 3:14) which God reveals as his name to Moses. It also means that *you* are named in the sense that you see yourself as one who is called by God by your name.

Your understanding of the divine Mystery behind it all is best expressed in terms like "glimpses" or "hints" for how deep are the riches and the wisdom and the knowledge of God.

> How rich are the depths of God—how deep his wisdom and knowledge—and how impossible to penetrate his motives or understand his methods! *Who could ever know the mind of the Lord? Who could ever be his counsellor? Who could ever give him anything or lend him anything?* (Romans 11:33-35)

A beginning of wisdom is to know and acknowledge that you do not know and that what you know falls far short of the Holy Mystery.

Living mystery not only says something about the unique person you are. It also says something about what

---

[43] Einstein, Albert, "What I Believe," *Forum*, October 1930.

you are called to be— to become more and more a living mystery to other people.

Your Life Story and Your Faith Story

Relationships of friendship and love rest upon faith. Faith enables one to say, in effect, to a friend or loved one, "I believe not only the things you are saying. I believe in you."

So also your relationship of love with the Holy Mystery we call God rests upon faith. When your life story includes in some way the story of your relationship with God, your life story can be described as your faith story. Your life story and your faith story are not two different stories. Your faith story *is* your life story expressed in the setting of your relationship with God.

Bernard Lonergan offers insight into faith and faith story by describing faith as "the eye of love."[44] As the eye is the organ of seeing, so also faith is the way of seeing love at work in one's own life, in relationships with others and in the world we inhabit. St. John reminds us, "...anyone who lives in love lives in God,..." (1 John 4:16). So when you tell your story in the light of love at work in your life, your life story becomes your faith story.

Questions for Reflection and Discussion

1) What are some examples of times when telling your story was important to you?

2) What are some examples of times when the inability to

[44] Lonergan, *Method in Theology*, p. 117.

tell your story was harmful to you?

3) What are some examples of times when telling your story helped you find meaning or give meaning to what's happening within you or around you?

4) What are some examples of times when telling your story meant turning pain into narrative in order to bear it?

5) What are some examples of times when telling your story meant turning happiness into narrative in order to prolong it?

6) What are some examples from your experience to illustrate that your life story is also your faith story?

7) What are some examples of "love at work" in your life?

Exercise

In the first two exercises you imagined and remembered your story. In this exercise you move from imagining your personal story to imagining your faith story by imagining your relationship with God.

St. Paul declares that Jesus is "...the image of the unseen God" (Colossians 1:15). In this exercise you use your imagination to picture your relationship with Jesus.

You visualize him present with you. St. Teresa of Avila said she was unable to visualize herself speaking to Jesus "eye-to-eye." She visualized him by her side. You visualize him, surrounded by light, present with you.

There are three variations of this visualizing which may be described as "Jesus within you," "Jesus at your side" and "Jesus in front of you." In the first you visualize his presence within you by seeing yourself surrounded with light and radiating the light of his presence.

In the second you visualize Jesus at your side either by visualizing his physical presence surrounded by light or by visualizing radiant light, which is the light of his presence with you. In the third you visualize yourself on a path and a being of light is ahead of you at the end of that path. The being of light is Jesus drawing you to himself. Each step you take brings you closer to Jesus.

Next, become aware that these three variations are not exclusive. Each complements and supports the others. You can move easily from one variation to the other. The form of visualizing that makes prayer easier for you is the one you stay with. At any moment you may choose to change from one form of visualizing to another. Your life story is now your faith story as you acknowledge in prayer that you do not walk alone.

Suggestions for Further Study, Reflection and Exploration

1) John Shea's *Stories of God* (Chicago: Thomas More Press, 1978) focuses upon the stories of God in the Old and New Testament. He places them under specific themes: stories of hope and justice, stories of trust and freedom, stories of invitation and decision.

2) Anthony de Mello's *The Song of the Bird* (New York, N.Y.: Doubleday and Co., Inc., 1984) begins with a distinction between theology and mysticism. He describes theology as the art of telling stories and listening to stories about the Divine. He describes mysticism as the art of relishing the stories to the point

that they transform us. The book consists of one-page stories, most of which are followed by short comments.

Chapter Four

Ways of Telling Your Story

You awaken your memory when you look upon your life as a story. You can describe your story in different ways. You can remember things you have done, goals and objectives that you have achieved. In this case the emphasis is upon what you have done and your story becomes what Dunne calls a "story of deeds."[45]

You can also look upon your story as one of experience, a story of all that you have lived through. In this case the emphasis is upon what you have felt and your story becomes what Dunne calls a "story of experience."

You can also look upon your story as one of self-growth and self-development. In this instance the emphasis is less upon your deeds or your feelings and more on your "self"—what Dunne, borrowing a term from Martin Heidigger, calls a "story of self-realization."

You can learn something about yourself from each of these ways of looking upon your life—a story of deeds, a story of experience and a story of self-realization—as long as you are mindful that each has strengths and limitations. Each way of telling your story is valid, but each story is not the whole story.

---

[45] Dunne, *A Search for God in Time and Memory.*

A Story of Deeds

One of the strengths involved in looking upon your story as a story of deeds is that it emphasizes the place of action in your life. Jesus' words, "If you love me you will keep my commandments" (John 14:15), indicate that one criterion for demonstrating love is to be found in what we do or do not do.

To look upon your life as a story of deeds does not mean that the deeds must be spectacular or heroic. Far more often the deeds are the actions involved in the ordinary giving to and receiving from others that constitute your daily life.

Dunne speaks of these actions:

> Giving and receiving have some role in every life. Together they constitute what could be called "love" in a life, if we understand love in terms of action more than in terms of feeling. The moral of the life of Jesus, in his own words, would be "Love one another as I have loved you." Loving as he loved would mean giving to others whatever one has from God, not receiving testimony or honor from others, and yet receiving the others who are given to one by God.... It would mean not being received by many, being received by a few, and giving what one has to those few.... The willingness to receive of which we have been speaking is a willingness to be influenced by others. When one is willingly influenced by others however, one is not controlled by them.[46]

In the life of Jesus we find giving *and* receiving. We usually think of the life of Jesus only in terms of giving; we rarely think of his life in terms of receiving. He did not receive such tangibles as wealth, honors, worldly power and prestige. His receiving was at a deeper level, as he

---

[46] John S. Dunne, *The Way of All the Earth* (New York, N.Y.: Macmillan Co., 1972), p. 169.

received people into his life.

We sometimes think of the Christian ideal as a life of all giving and no receiving. Dunne points out that Jesus' life illustrates that it's not that way. There's a danger involved in an attitude of all giving and no receiving. The danger is that if you don't acknowledge a receiving side to your life, you may more easily become a taker. Indeed, one description of sinning is the taking of that which is not given or the taking of that which may not be given.

Dunne makes a distinction between being controlled by others and being influenced by others. To be influenced by others means to let them be present to us, to be open to them, to receive from them.

Jesus received by receiving people into his life in various ways. He received a number of women into his life, as well as their financial help: "With him went the Twelve, as well as certain women who had been cured of evil spirits and ailments: Mary surnamed the Magdalene, from whom seven demons had gone out, Joanna the wife of Herod's steward Chuza, Susanna, and several others who provided for them out of their own resources" (Luke 8:1-3).

Jesus received Zacchaeus and Zacchaeus' hospitality: "Hurry, because I must stay at your house today" (Luke 19:6).

He received the woman who approached him in the house of Simon the Pharisee. He received her affection to the chagrin of his host who "said to himself, 'If this man were a prophet, he would know who this woman is that is touching him and what a bad name she has'" (Luke 7:39). Jesus was not controlled by others but he was willing to be influenced by them. He was willing to receive from them.

Dunne cites St. Paul as an example of one who looked upon life as a story of deeds. Prior to his conversion to

Christianity he saw deeds as necessary for salvation; after his conversion he saw the inadequacy of deeds alone for salvation. In each instance deeds become the basis of the life story: in one instance their necessity, in the other their inadequacy.

The Letter of St. James provides a scriptural basis for seeing one's life as a story of deeds:

> If one of the brothers or one of the sisters is in need of clothes and has not enough food to live on, and one of you says to them, "I wish you well; keep yourself warm and eat plenty," without giving them these bare necessities of life, then what good is that? Faith is like that: if good works do not go with it, it is quite dead.... A body dies when it is separated from the spirit, and in the same way faith is dead if it is separated from good deeds. (James 2:15-17, 26)

One of the limitations involved in looking upon one's story as a story of deeds is that deeds alone are not enough. More important than what you do is the reason you do them. The motives and the intentions behind the deeds are so important that a faulty motive can diminish the best of deeds and an evil motive can corrupt the best of deeds. As T.S. Eliot expresses it in *Murder in the Cathedral*,

> The last temptation is the greatest treason:
> To do the right deed for the wrong reason.[47]

St. Paul explores both the strength and the limitation of deeds in his First Letter to the Corinthians, chapters twelve and thirteen. He begins by speaking at length of various gifts, talents and abilities which God gives to his people. He indicates that the gifts given to each are to be used for the good of all. He speaks of the importance of doing all those things that one is called to do. Then he begins on the

---

[47] T.S. Eliot, *Murder in the Cathedral, The Complete Poems and Plays* (New York, N.Y.: Harcourt, Brace & World, Inc., 1962), p. 196.

subject of the inadequacy of deeds alone, "...I am going to show you a way that is better than any of them" (1 Corinthians 12:31).

He proceeds to imagine some of the most dazzling, extraordinary, heroic deeds possible. He spells them out: speaking with the tongues of men and angels, having faith strong enough to move mountains, giving away everything to feed the poor, undergoing the death of a martyr. He indicates that if you do or undergo all of them and have not love, they all add up to nothing.

Anthony de Mello uses a format of dialogue between the master and the disciple to illustrate that deeds (in this example referred to as "spiritual exercises"), while ineffective in themselves to bring one closer to God, are still important,

> "Is there anything I can do to make myself Enlightened?"
> "As little as you can do to make the sun rise in the morning."
> "Then of what use are the spiritual exercises you prescribe?"
> "To make sure you are not asleep when the sun begins to rise."[48]

Both the strength and limitation of looking upon your life as a story of deeds is illustrated in St. Luke's account of Martha and her sister, Mary:

> In the course of their journey he came to a village, and a woman named Martha welcomed him into her house. She had a sister called Mary, who sat down at the Lord's feet and listened to him speaking. Now Martha who was distracted with all the serving said, "Lord, do you not care that my sister is leaving me to do the serving all by myself? Please tell her to help

---

[48] Anthony de Mello, *One Minute Wisdom* (Garden City, N.Y.: Doubleday and Co., Inc., 1986), back cover.

me." But the Lord answered: "Martha, Martha," he
said, "you worry and fret about so many things, and
yet few are needed, indeed only one. It is Mary who
has chosen the better part; it is not to be taken from
her." (Luke 10:38-42)

Martha and Mary can be looked upon as representing
two aspects of the Christian life. Martha stands for deeds,
service to others, busy with the preparation of a meal. Mary
stands for presence to another, listening, being attentive.
Martha stands for doing; Mary stands for being.

Martha represents prayer translated into action. Mary
represents prayer as being in the presence of the God who
loves us. Martha stands for what we do; Mary stands for
what we are.

Anne Morrow Lindbergh speaks of what we might
describe as the "Martha-Mary tension":

> Total retirement is not possible. I cannot shed my
> responsibilities. I cannot permanently inhabit a desert
> island. I cannot be a nun in the midst of family life. I
> would not want to be. The solution for me, surely, is
> neither in total renunciation of the world, nor in total
> acceptance of it. I must find a balance somewhere, or
> an alternating rhythm between these two
> extremes;...between solitude and communication,
> between retreat and return.[49]

What we do is important. It's important because it's part
of what we are. However, what we are matters more than
what we do, as Jesus says to Martha, "It is Mary who has
chosen the better part" (Luke 10:42).

However, your task is not to choose one or the
other—Martha or Mary. In the words of St. Teresa of Avila,
"To give our Lord a perfect hospitality Mary and Martha

---

[49] Anne Morrow Lindbergh, *Gift From the Sea* (New York, N.Y.: Pantheon
Books, 1955), p. 30.

must combine."[50] Rather, your task is to bring what each represents into your life, to seek some kind of balance between them. The balance is achieved when Martha's action proceeds from love and Mary's attentiveness proceeds from love.

A Story of Experience

In addition to looking upon your life as a story of deeds, you may also look upon your life with an emphasis upon what you have experienced, what you have undergone, what you have felt. Your story as a story of experience includes some expression of your feelings. One of the strengths involved in looking upon your life in this way is that the story of experience includes not only your actions but also your reactions and feelings about those actions.

As Bernard Lonergan notes, "We have feelings about other persons, we feel for them, we feel with them. We have feelings about our respective situations, about the past, about the future, about evils to be lamented or remedied, about the good that can, must be accomplished."[51]

Marcel Proust speaks of "our true life" as "reality as we have felt it to be."[52] This is not to say that feeling is everything or that feeling is the only thing. One need not agree with Goethe's Faust that "feeling is all."[53] It is to say that feelings and the story of one's feelings have a rightful place as a basis for the telling of one's story.

---

[50] Teresa of Avila, *Interior Castle* (Garden City, N.Y.: Doubleday and Co., Inc., 1961), p. 231.

[51] Lonergan, *Method in Theology*, p. 31.

[52] Proust, Vol. III, p. 915.

[53] Johann Wolfgang von Goethe, *Faust*, trans. Louis MacNeice (New York, N.Y.: Oxford University Press, 1951), p. 113.

A scriptural basis for looking upon one's life as a story of experience is found in the opening words of the First Letter of St. John,

> Something which has existed since the beginning,
> that we have heard,
> and we have seen with our own eyes;
> that we have watched
> and touched with our hands:
> the Word, who is life—
> .... What we have seen and heard
> we are telling you.... (1 John 1:1-3)

The writer emphasizes that it's what he has experienced, namely, seen, heard and touched, that he is telling them. He is telling them a story of personal experience. He trusts his own experience. That experience is the basis of what he has to say.

While the life of St. Paul suggests itself at first glance as a story of deeds, his life can also be looked upon as a story of experience, as evidenced in his letters. More than once he draws attention to his own personal experience, as, for example, when he indicates to the Corinthians some of the dangers he has faced, "...danger from rivers and in danger from brigands, in danger from my own people and in danger from pagans; in danger in the towns, in danger in the open country, danger at sea and danger from so-called brothers" (2 Corinthians 11:26).

He recounts his own personal feelings of anxiety, "...there is my daily preoccupation: my anxiety for all the churches" (2 Corinthians 11:28). He does not hesitate to speak of extraordinary experiences that have been a part of his life, "...I will move on to the visions and revelations I have had from the Lord" (2 Corinthians 12:1).

While not an eyewitness to the person of Jesus during his earthly life, Paul indicates that his experience of God revealing to him his Son gives him a credibility comparable to those apostles who knew Jesus during his lifetime. He presents his story as a story of his experience of what God has done for him, with him and in him.

John Dunne sees autobiographies in general and Augustine's *Confessions* in particular as examples of life looked upon as a story of experience. Of Augustine Dunne notes, "The story of his life has an archetypal quality about it because it is told as a story of experience,...rather than as a tale of unique deeds and achievements."[54]

In his autobiography, *Memories, Dreams, Reflections*, Carl Jung distinguishes between outward happenings and inner experience in his life,

> I speak chiefly of inner experiences.... All other memories of travels, people and my surroundings have paled beside these interior happenings.... Outward circumstances are no substitute for inner experience:...my life has been singularly poor in outward happenings.... I can understand myself only in the light of inner happenings.[55]

One reason for the attraction we find in autobiography as well as in any good story is that it is usually more than a chronicle of deeds. In a story there is a meeting of two worlds: the world of the writer who is revealing in some way his inner world of experience and the world of the reader who has an inner world of his own. In the words of Robert Doran, " 'Who I am' is a far more extensive and rich story of experiences, feelings, insights, judgments, decisions and religious commitments than 'what I do.' "[56]

Martin Buber contrasts the inner world of one's own

[54] Dunne, *The Way of All the Earth*, p. xii.
[55] Jung, *Memories, Dreams, Reflections*, pp. 4-5.
[56] Robert M. Doran, "Jungian Psychology and Christian Spirituality," *Review for Religious*, Volume 38, 1979, Article II, p. 747.

experience with the outer world:

> Institutions are "outside," where all sorts of aims are
> pursued, where a [person] works, negotiates, bears
> influence, undertakes, concurs, organizes, conducts
> business.... Feelings are "within," where life is lived
> and man recovers from institutions. Here the
> spectrum of the emotions dances before the
> interested glance.

> Here one's liking and hate and pleasure are
> indulged.... Here he is at home, and stretches himself
> out in his rocking chair.[57]

Your experience, good and bad, pleasant and painful,
wise and foolish, can be the raw material for greater
self-understanding, if you bring those experiences to your
intellect. In the words of Anthony de Mello,

> The Master was an advocate both of learning and of
> Wisdom.
> "Learning," he said when asked, "is gotten by reading
> books or listening to lectures."
> "And Wisdom?"
> "By reading the book that is you."[58]

Marcel Proust speaks of the importance of bringing
what you have felt and experienced within the range of the
light of your mind:

> Certainly what I had felt in my hours of love is what all
> men feel. One feels, yes, but what one feels is like a
> negative which shows only blackness until one has
> placed it near a special lamp and which also must be
> looked at in reverse. So with one's feelings: Until one
> has brought them within range of the intellect, one
> does not know what they represent. Then only, when
> the intellect has shed light upon them, has
> intellectualized them, does one distinguish, and with

[57] Martin Buber, *I and Thou*, trans. Ronald Gregor Smith (New York, N.Y.:
Charles Scribner's Sons, 1958), p. 43.
[58] de Mello, p. 177.

what difficulty, the lineaments of what one felt.[59]

In similar fashion John Dunne discovers the insight in experience when on a journey to investigate the religions of the east.

> Originally I expected that experiments with truth would mean gaining new experiences by walking new paths.... As I went on, though, I began to realize that the experiences on which the religions were based were common experiences, and that the uncommon thing was the insight into the experiences, the "enlightenment" and the "revelation."[60]

Robert Doran speaks of this experience as "psychic conversion" as "knowing what one is feeling: of being able to tell one's story, and to tell it as it is."[61] In commenting upon the work of Bernard Lonergan, Doran speaks of the importance of insight into "ordinary" experience,

> Lonergan emphasizes that spiritual development is not something that occurs in some realm that is isolated from the insights that we have into the events of our everyday life, from the judgments that we make as to the truth or falsity of the most mundane propositions, from the anxieties we feel and the decisions that we make regarding our orientation and actions as beings in-the-world.
>
> God's saving purpose is a will to save the world itself, to redeem the time of our lives, as Eliot would put it. It is not a dimension of reality that is totally extrinsic from the events of understanding, judging and deciding, that we experience every day.[62]

However, one of the limitations of your story as one of experience is the fact that experience can be the raw material for self-deception as well as self-understanding,

[59] Proust, Vol. III, p. 933.
[60] Dunne, *The Way of All the Earth*, p. xii.
[61] Doran, Article I, p. 505.
[62] Doran, Article I, pp. 500-501.

self-delusion as well as self-knowledge. To gain insight from your experience is easier said than done. Proust speaks of the difficulty our minds have in shedding light upon our feelings. Doran speaks of knowing what one is feeling as attainable only through that process of change called conversion.

Just as there is no necessary connection between the passing of time in one's life and growth in wisdom, so also there's no necessary connection between the gaining of experience and the gaining of wisdom from that experience. Thomas Merton offers an analysis of why it is so difficult for our minds to shed the kind of light on our experience that leads to wisdom:

> I think that if there is one truth that people need to learn, in the world, especially today, it is this: the intellect is only theoretically independent of desire and appetite in ordinary, actual practice. It is constantly being blinded and perverted by the ends and aims of passion, and the evidence it presents to us with such a show of impartiality and objectivity is fraught with interest and propaganda. We have become marvelous at self-delusion; all the more so, because we have gone to such trouble to convince ourselves of our own absolute infallibility. The desires of the flesh—and by that I mean not only sinful desires, but even the ordinary, normal appetites for comfort and ease and human respect, are fruitful sources of every kind of error and misjudgement, and because we have these yearnings in us, our intellects (which, if they operated all alone in a vacuum, would indeed, register with pure impartiality what they saw) present to us everything distorted and accommodated to the norms of our desire.[63]

T.S. Eliot speaks of the self-deceiving aspect of experience:

[63] Thomas Merton, *The Seven Storey Mountain* (New York, N.Y.: Harcourt Brace Jovanovich, 1948), p. 205.

There is, it seems to us,
At best only a limited value
In the knowledge derived from experience.
The knowledge imposes a pattern, and falsifies,
For the pattern is new in every moment
And every moment is a new and shocking
Valuation of all we have been.[64]

Your experience can become a closed system in which you refuse to be a learner and a listener. If you do not acknowledge the incompleteness of your experience as well as the incompleteness of your understanding of your experience, you are less likely to grow beyond it.

A Story of Self

John Dunne sees the modern life story taking yet another form in which your life story is looked upon as a story of self, as illustrated in a number of ways.

I've already noted the present popularity of referring to your self-image, the importance of the picture or image of yourself that you have.

Note the recurrence of the word "self" in common words: self-affirmation, self-respect, self-help, self-assertion, self-enrichment, self-improvement. Each indicates an act or a process which places the self at the center. In some cases, the self is active as a doer, moving in the direction of, for example, assertion, enrichment and improvement. In other cases, the self is passive, as a recipient, for example, of acceptance and affirmation.

The story of self has a scriptural basis in the words of Jesus, "...You must love the Lord your God with all your heart, with all your soul, and with all your mind. This is the

---

[64] Eliot, *Murder in the Cathedral*, p. 125.

greatest and the first commandment. The second resembles it: You must love your neighbor as yourself" (Matthew 22:37-39).

However, you cannot "love your neighbor as yourself" until you first of all have a self to give. Therefore, your story as a story of self is a valid and important way of looking upon your life story. It reminds you that growth in self-understanding plays a part in achieving the growth you are called to as a human person.

This emphasis upon self, these many forms of self-realization, far from being a form of selfishness, are a necessary starting point for responding to other human beings in a non-exploitative way. How often it happens that when we harm ourselves or harm another human being and we know that we have done so, we say to ourselves, "I just wasn't myself when I did that. It just wasn't me." It is in striving toward personal ideals that we find ourselves and become ourselves.

In the same way when we surrender personal ideals, we may somehow surrender our "self" in a harmful way. When we surrender personal ideals, we may somehow wave good-bye to something we recognize as good within us.

This kind of self-realization has received one of its classic statements in the words of Shakespeare's Polonius in *Hamlet*:

> This above all—to thine own self be true,
> And it must follow, as the night the day,
> Thou canst not then be false to any man.[65]

Thomas Merton speaks of self-realization,

> Freedom from domination, freedom to live one's own spiritual life, freedom to seek the highest truth, unabashed by any human pressure or any collective

[65] Shakespeare, *Hamlet*, I, iii, 78-80.

demand, the ability to say one's own "yes" and one's own "no" and not merely to echo the "yes" and the "no" of state, party, corporation, army or system. This is inseparable from authentic religion. It is one of the deepest and most fundamental needs of man, perhaps the deepest and most crucial need of the human person as such.[66]

The story of self-realization, looking upon one's life as a story of self, is not the whole story of Christian living but rather an important starting point. Christian living does not end with oneself, but it does begin with oneself.

Robert Doran, a Jungian psychologist, states that Jungian psychology can help our understanding of some aspects of the Christian tradition. He says there is a "parting of the ways" between Jungian psychology and the Christian tradition on the subject of "self":

> Regarding "the still point" Christian tradition does not call it the self. It declares emphatically that the "still point" is not just me, but is rather the region where God dwells in my inmost being. The innermost region of our interiority is, in the Christian mystical tradition, no longer ourselves but the place of grace, where the gift of God's love is poured forth into our hearts by the Holy Spirit Who has been given to us. It is what Lonergan calls "the region of the divine."[67]

Hence, the limitation in looking upon your life as a story of "self" is that it leaves your life story incomplete. Self-acceptance and self-affirmation are necessary aspects of your growth as a person, but they leave untold a further aspect of your story, what may be called a "story beyond self," namely, your relationships with others.

That limitation on your story as a story of self is expressed in Victor Hugo's novel *Les Miserables*. Jean

[66] Thomas Merton, *Conjectures of a Guilty Bystander* (Garden City, N.Y.: Doubleday and Co., Inc., 1968), p. 59.
[67] Doran, Article III, p. 861.

Valjean is facing a decision that will have enormous personal consequences for him: keep quiet about his past and watch an innocent person go to prison or tell the truth and incriminate himself. Hugo expresses Valjean's reflection in this way, "He had, it seems, concluded, after the manner of saints and sages, that his first duty was not to himself."[68]

The story beyond self can be described as the story of self and soul. Traditionally, a distinction is made between *body* and soul. However, in Yeats' poem, "A Dialogue of Self and Soul," the distinction is between *self* and soul.[69] John Dunne suggests that the untold story in the story of "self" is the story of "soul." In other words, you not only have a self, but also you have a soul. You not only are a self, but also you are a soul.

Dunne explains the difference between self and soul by using the imagery of light and darkness. He begins by comparing our personal lifetime to a period of light in contrast with the darkness that existed before we were born and the darkness that will exist after we have died. Self is that in us that loves the brightness of our lifetime. Soul is that in us that loves the darkness from which we have come and toward which we are moving. God dwells both in the brightness of our lifetime and in the darkness that precedes and follows our lifetime. With all the present emphasis upon self, there also needs to be room for a "story beyond self" or a "story of soul" for as Dunne notes, "[M]an does not live by self alone."[70]

---

[68] Victor Hugo, *Les Miserables* (New York, N.Y.: Penguin Books, 1976), p. 209.

[69] William B. Yeats, "A Dialogue of Self and Soul," *The Collected Poems of W.B. Yeats* (New York, N.Y.: Macmillan Co., 1972), p. 230.

[70] Dunne, *A Search for God in Time and Memory*, p. 205.

Questions for Reflection, Discussion

1) In what way do you prefer to tell your story: a story of deeds, a story of experience, a story of self?

2) In looking upon your life as a story of deeds what are some examples of giving and receiving that are so much a part of your life you scarcely think about them?

3) What are some examples in which failing to acknowledge a receiving side to your life could incline you to become a "taker"?

4) What are some examples from your life of Dunne's distinction between being controlled by others and being influenced by them?

5) What are some examples in your life of doing "the right deed for the wrong reason"?

6) What are some examples in your life of the "Mary-Martha tension"?

7) What are some examples of gaining insight and understanding from your experience?

8) What are some examples in which your experience was a source of self-deception?

Exercise

This exercise begins in a way similar to the exercise in Chapter Three except that here Mary, the mother of Jesus, is the one whom you visualize. In the New Testament God is portrayed for the most part through male imagery.

The presence of Mary, the mother of Jesus, helps

restore a masculine-feminine balance in religion. She is a doorway of connection to God as Woman, God as Mother.

This exercise is one that goes beyond the visualizing of Jesus and/or Mary and the prayer that such visualizing may inspire. It can be called the exercise of *fiat*, a Latin word meaning "let it be done," "let it happen," or in specifically religious language, "thy will be done."

Since fiat is a brief word containing much meaning, you can use it as a kind of mantra whose slow repetition quiets you down and places you in the presence of the One.

There are times when you are active in prayer, expressing particular needs for yourself and/or others. There are times when you are active in prayer, expressing particular sentiments such as gratitude and praise.

There are also times when you are passive in prayer and called to be passive. You can describe these times as the times you are called to fiat. These are the times of prayer "with no agenda," times of listening, times of waiting. Don't try to activate yourself at these times; just let yourself be. Let go. Let your prayer be fiat. Let yourself be led.

If you decide you need more words in prayer, you can use the longer form of fiat, Mary's own words, "...let what you have said be done to me" (Luke 1:38). Let what surfaces, surface. Don't be surprised that it takes effort and practice to "let yourself be." Trust the One who is leading you, especially when by your standards, "nothing is happening." Be still. Let go.

In the Chapter Three exercise your life story becomes your faith story as you move into the presence of God through prayer. The emphasis there is upon prayer as something you do. In this exercise the emphasis is upon prayer as something that is done to you and within you. The previous exercise emphasizes your action in prayer.

This exercise emphasizes God's action in prayer. Part of the process called discernment in prayer is the act of learning when and how to give to each its proper emphasis, when to let go of prayer as doing and to move into prayer as "Let it happen, your will be done."

Suggestions for Further Study, Reflection and Exploration

1) One way of telling one's story is through a diary or journal. Dag Hammarskjöld's *Markings* (New York: Alfred A. Knopf, Inc., 1964) is comprised of his diary entries from 1925 to 1961. It does not contain a single reference to his career as an international civil servant and Secretary General of the United Nations.

2) At more than twice the length of *Markings* is *Journal of a Soul* (New York: McGraw-Hill, 1965), the autobiography of Angelo Roncalli, Pope John XXIII. Following a format of journal entries, *Journal of a Soul* begins in seminary days in 1895 and concludes in 1963.

3) *Spiritual Quests* (Boston: Houghton Mifflin, 1988) is subtitled "The Art and Craft of Religious Writing." Six American writers from different religious faith backgrounds—Mary Gordon, David Bradley, Jaroslav Pelikan, Frederick Buechner, Hugh Nissenson and Allen Ginsburg—describe how spiritual concerns influence their life stories and their writings.

Chapter Five

Listening to the
Stories of Others

Listening to Others

If you have a sense of reverence and respect for yourself as the mystery you are, you also need reverence and respect for others as the mystery they are. John Dunne speaks of passing over from one's own life and standpoint to the life and standpoint of other people, learning from their lives and then returning to one's own life enriched.

This process becomes an ever-deepening exploration of mystery. "...[O]ur searcher, as he goes from one person to another, always finds what he is looking for, since each person is inexhaustible, each is a mystery, but he continues searching, nevertheless, because the further he goes, the more light is shed upon the mystery."[71]

Works of Fiction: Shedding Light on the Mystery of Ourselves

Part of the fascination that works of fiction, the stories of others, hold for us lies in the fact that a story, like an

---

[71] Dunne, *A Search for God in Time and Memory*, p. 7.

image, can have more than one meaning. A good story gives us "room to move around in," room in which to bring our own life experience to bear. In understanding the inner world of someone else through a story, you may come to a better understanding of your own inner world.

In the words of Saul Bellow,

> I think that fiction still has more to tell people than non-fiction. I think that we are being swallowed up by journalism and discourse. There are so many books that are written just for the head and don't address feelings at all. A good novel does address feelings. It engages you one to one; you and the writer together share something, share a sense of life.[72]

The relationship between a story and the personal world of the reader is expressed by Marcel Proust as he reflects upon the relationship between his readers and himself as an author:

> I thought more modestly of my book and it would be inaccurate even to say that I thought of those who would read it as "my" readers. For it seemed to me that they would not be "my" readers but the readers of their own selves, my book being merely a sort of magnifying glass...it would be my book but with its help I would furnish them with the means of reading what lay within themselves.
>
> So that I should not ask them to praise me or censure me but simply to tell me whether it really is like that. I should ask them whether the words they read within themselves are the same as those which I have written.[73]

Proust speaks not only of the "magnifying glass" or the "mirror quality" of favorite stories or favorite works of art but also of the "mirror quality" of those who produce them, those

[72] Saul Bellow in an interview for *Book of the Month Club News*, Book of the Month Club, Inc.; Camp Hill, Pa. Summer 1987, p. 5.
[73] Proust, Vol. III, p. 1089.

...who produce works of genius are not those who live in the most delicate atmosphere, whose conversation is the most brilliant or their culture the most extensive, but those who have had the power, ceasing suddenly to live only for themselves, to transform their personality into a sort of mirror, in such a way that their life, however mediocre it may be...is reflected by it, genius consisting in reflecting power and not in the intrinsic quality of the scene reflected.[74]

The mirror quality is also seen in the instance of a great artist "in action":

With a great musician...his playing is that of so fine a pianist that one is no longer aware that the performer is a pianist at all, because...his playing has become so transparent, so imbued with what he is interpreting, that one no longer sees the performer himself—he is simply a window opening upon a great work of art.[75]

Shakespeare offers a classic statement of the work of art in general and the play in particular fulfilling the function of a mirror, in Hamlet's advice to the players, "[T]he purpose of playing whose end, both at the first and now, was and is to hold as 'twere the mirror up to nature, to show virtue her own feature, scorn her own image, and the very age and body of this time his form and pressure."[76]

Hence, the stories that mean the most to us tend to be not so much those that speak to us only about other people or the world around us. Our favorites tend to be those that speak to us about ourselves, those that in some way become, in Shakespeare's words, a "mirror," in Proust's words, a "magnifying glass," in which we see a reflection of ourselves and our personal story, our own personal drama. In the words of Anthony de Mello, "You have yet to

---

[74] Proust, Vol. I, p. 597.
[75] Proust, Vol, II, pp. 43, 44.
[76] Shakespeare, *Hamlet*, III, ii, 20-24.

understand...that the shortest distance between a human being and Truth is a story."[77]

When you say, for example, that a story "rings true" or "doesn't ring true," what you're saying is that the story does or does not bear truth for your experience and understanding of life. The criterion or yardstick for measuring is personal, namely, what this story means to you, your personal reaction to it. You may not be able to describe or analyze your reaction to a story. You may only know that "I like it" or "I don't like it."

As Henry James said, "Nothing, of course, will ever take the place of the good old fashion of 'liking' a work of art or not liking it: the most improved criticism will not abolish that primitive, that ultimate test."[78]

In speaking of a story as a way of reading what lies within oneself, Proust adds to the imagery of a magnifying glass that of different kinds of lenses. The lenses can be compared to the different kinds of stories we encounter, each of which has the purpose of making it easier for you to understand, not so much someone else, but rather yourself:

> For it is only out of habit, a habit contracted from the insincere language of prefaces and dedications that the writer speaks of 'my reader.' In reality every reader is, while he is reading, the reader of his own self. The writer's book is merely a kind of optical instrument which he offers to the reader to enable him to discern what, without this book, he would perhaps never have perceived in himself....
>
> In order to read with understanding many readers require to read in their own particular fashion, and the author must not be indignant at this; on the contrary, he must leave the reader all possible liberty, saying to

[77] de Mello, p. 23.
[78] Henry James, "The Art of Fiction," *Criticism: Twenty Major Statements* (Scranton: Chandler Publishing Co., year of publication not indicated) p. 432.

him, "Look for yourself, and try whether you see best with this lens or that one or this other one."[79]

Proust indicates that when you make a discovery while reading a story, the discovery resides not so much in the story but rather within you by means of the story. When you find "something new" in a story, the "something new" is in you by means of the story. The story hasn't changed; you've changed.

Questions for Reflection and Discussion

1) What are some examples from your life in which listening to the stories of others has changed your life?

2) What are some of the novels, plays, movies that have meant the most to you, that are your favorites? Why?

3) Was it only the content of the work of art itself that makes it one of your favorites or was the work of art combined with other factors, e.g., what was happening in your life at the time?

4) What are some examples from your experience of artists so imbued with what they are interpreting that they are simply window openings upon great works of art, as Proust says?

5) When is the last time you thanked God for Mozart or Shakespeare or Beethoven or your personal list of artists who have touched/changed your life?

[79] Proust, Vol. III, p. 949.

Exercise

Choose three favorite works of fiction, be they novels, plays or movies.

If you are in a group, explain what about these three makes them your favorites. In doing so, do not limit yourself to talking about the work of fiction itself. Connect the work of fiction with yourself and with your story. Explain how the work of fiction has influenced you now and/or at different times in your life. In this way you are explaining the ways in which you have made the work of art your own.

A variation of this exercise is to choose another kind of work of art such as a music composition, perhaps a favorite symphony, or a favorite painting. Tell what this symphony or painting means to you. Tell the ways in which you have made this symphony or painting your own.

If you are doing this exercise alone, write down your responses to each of the above steps. In either case, whether alone or with others, the emphasis here is not primarily upon the work of art but rather upon your personal connection with the work of art. This emphasis will prevent the discussion or the writing from turning into a discussion or a writing of the relative merits of various works of art. It is your relationship with the work of art that is the focus.

**Suggestions for Further Study,
Reflection and Exploration**

1) *Once a Catholic: Prominent Catholics and Ex-Catholics Reveal the Influence of the Church on Their Lives and Work,* (ed. Peter Occhiogrosso, Boston: Houghton

Mifflin Co., 1987) provides examples of looking to one's religious past—in this book one's Catholic past—as an essential ingredient of telling one's story. It is based on interviews with twenty-six Catholics who offer a look at how the Catholic experience has influenced their lives.

2) In developing his themes related to religious experience in his book, *The Varieties of Religious Experience: A Study in Human Nature* (New York: Macmillan Co., 1961), William James includes the stories of the religious experiences of numbers of people, most of whose religious roots are in Christianity.

3) *The Little Prince* by Antoine de Saint Exupery (New York: Harcourt Brace Jovanovich, 1968) is a children's story that has something to say to others besides children. In the course of his travels the Little Prince meets a fox from whom he learns what is really important in life.

Chapter Six

Imagining Your Past

Your Life Is a Walk Up a Mountain

Your life may be looked upon as a gradual, ongoing
process like climbing a mountain. An example is the
gradual ascent of the mountain of purgatory, described in
Dante's *Divine Comedy*. Your life may also be looked upon
in terms of sacred moments. In this case your life may be
compared to going to the top of a mountain periodically for
sacred moments and then returning to the valley of your
day-by-day existence.

At times, if you view your life in terms of sacred
moments, everything that happened before a special
moment may be seen as a preparation for it; everything that
happened after it may be seen as flowing from it.

Indeed, your life may be looked upon both as the
ongoing climbing of a mountain as well as the periodic
ascent of a mountain and the return to the valley.

By way of imagery you visualize the original sacred
moment as your being on a mountaintop. You visualize
your remembrance of the original sacred moment as your
return to the same mountaintop, the mountaintop revisited,
the mountaintop regained.

Sacred Moment: The Mountain in Scripture

You can learn about the sacred moments in your own life through the imagery of the mountain by looking at some sacred moments in biblical times that are connected with the mountain image. In both the Old and New Testaments sacred moments are often linked with the imagery of a mountain. The mountain is often a place of meeting between God and human beings.

It is on Mount Sinai that God reveals himself to Moses in the burning bush as "...the God of your father,...the God of Abraham, the God of Isaac and the God of Jacob" (Exodus 3:6). It is on this same Mount Sinai that God gives the commandments to Moses. Chapters nineteen and twenty of the Book of Exodus, which describe this event, have been described as the heart of the first five books of the Bible. Everything before them may be seen as a preparation for them; everything following may be seen as flowing from them.

In the words of Andrew Greeley,

> The nineteenth chapter of Exodus makes it as clear as possible to us that we are dealing with a mighty and profound religious experience.... What was revealed in the twentieth chapter of Exodus was the revelation of God's loving care for His people.... God made a covenant,...and the world was changed.[80]

The content of the commandments was not new to the Israelites. What was new was the relationship of love and commitment (covenant) on the part of God with his people.

For the prophet Elijah a sacred time in his life is connected with a mountain. An angel of the Lord appears to him, provides him with food and indicates a journey Elijah

---

[80] Andrew M. Greeley, *The Sinai Myth* (Garden City, N.Y.: Doubleday and Co., Inc., 1972), pp. 44, 68.

is to undertake, "So he got up and ate and drank, and strengthened by that food he walked for forty days and forty nights until he reached Horeb, the mountain of God" (l Kings 19:8). It is on the mountaintop in the stillness of a quiet breeze that Elijah receives from God the enlightenment and revelation that will give direction to his life for years to come.

The Gospel accounts provide us with examples of the mountain in the life of Jesus: the Sermon on the Mount (Matthew 5:3-7), his transfiguration on Mount Tabor (Matthew 17:1-8), his prayer on the night before his death on the Mount of Olives (Mark 14:26-42), his death on Mount Calvary (Matthew 27:33-50), his ascension into heaven from the Mount of Olives (Matthew 28:16-20). In the words of Evelyn Underhill, "To go up alone into the mountain and come back as an ambassador to the world, has ever been the method of humanity's best friends."[81]

The mountain is a sign not only of sacred moments in the lives of individuals but also of sacred moments in the lives of all people. The prophet Isaiah foresees,

> In days to come,
> the mountain of the temple of Yahweh
> shall tower above the mountains....
> All the nations will stream to it,...
> and...say:
> "Come, let us go up to the mountain of Yahweh,...
> that he may teach us his ways
> so that we may walk in his paths;...." (Isaiah 2:2-3)

The mountain becomes a sign not only of sacred moments in the past but also sacred moments in the future.

The author of the Letter to the Hebrews speaks of the mountain that his listeners have already arrived at, "...what

---

[81] Evelyn Underhill, *Mysticism* (New York, N.Y.: E.P. Dutton and Co., Inc., 1961), p. 173.

you have come to is Mount Zion and the city of the living God, the heavenly Jerusalem where the millions of angels have gathered for the festival,.... You have come to God himself, the supreme Judge,...and to Jesus, the mediator who brings a new covenant,..." (Hebrews 12:22-24).

The author uses the present tense to describe his listeners' relationship to the mountain, saying in effect, "You are already there. You have already arrived at the mountain where God is." The implication is, "You don't have to travel further. You're already there at the place of the sacred moment. What remains is for you to become aware and to acknowledge that the present moment you reside in *is* a sacred moment. The sacred moment is each moment for those who have eyes to see."

Sacred Moments: Remembering the Mountain Through Scripture

The remembering and imagining of your personal past through the imagery of the mountain can be illumined by examples from Scripture. In Scripture we find descriptions not only of sacred moments but also the remembering of sacred moments.

When Moses is near death, he calls upon the people to remember the Sinai event, to remember its meaning, to let their lives in the present and future continue to be transformed by that experience of love, "...it was not because you outnumbered other peoples: you were the least of all peoples. It was for love of you..." (Deuteronomy 7:7-8).

He is assuming that this transforming moment in their past can be a transforming moment in their lives at the present moment. He stresses the uniqueness of that sacred moment in their lives, that divine breakthrough, "Was there ever a word so majestic, from one end of heaven to the other? Was anything ever heard? Did ever a people hear the voice of the living God speaking from the heart of the fire, as you heard it, and remain alive?" (Deuteronomy 4:32-33).

Moses is not only reminding the people of a sacred moment in their lives. He is also calling upon them to engage in a special kind of remembering, a remembering to involve not just their memories but their minds and hearts as well. He is calling upon them to remember that they are loved.

The evangelists describe the profound religious experience of Peter, James and John on Mount Tabor as they see Jesus transfigured before them, with Moses and Elijah appearing with him. It was an experience that would sustain them during some of the dark days to come at the time of Jesus' death. It was an experience that became for them a timeless moment in their lives—timeless in the sense that through their memories they could make that moment present to themselves again and again.

Peter relives that moment many years later when he speaks in his second epistle: "We heard this ourselves, spoken from heaven, when we were with him on the holy mountain" (2 Peter 1:18).

So, too, with ourselves the special moments in our lives that we often consider to be "past and over with" are not over. Through our memory a special moment in our past can become present to us again.

At times a special moment in our past becomes more than present to us. At times our memory of a past experience may move us and motivate us more deeply than did the original experience. The memory of a past experience may have more meaning for us than did the original experience.

In just the same way, Peter does more than relive the past moment of Jesus' transfiguration. He has an understanding of the past experience which he did not have at the time of the experience itself. In the light of Jesus' Resurrection, his transfiguration months earlier is better understood. Hence, Jesus' words on Mount Tabor now, in remembrance, make sense, "Tell no one about the vision until the Son of Man has risen from the dead" (Matthew 17:9).

The Mountain: Thomas Merton

In Thomas Merton's life, we can trace the image of climbing a mountain through successive stages in his life. We can also see the process of Merton making the image of the mountain "his own." He uses that image as a way of casting light upon his life—the life he has lived, the life he is living and the life he intends to live.

It is in the classroom at Cambridge that Merton becomes acquainted with Dante's *Divine Comedy*, which describes the poet's journey through hell, purgatory and heaven. The poet, Virgil, accompanies Dante in his journey through hell and purgatory; a woman named Beatrice is his companion in his journey through paradise. The journey through purgatory consists of the climbing of a seven-circled or seven storey mountain.

Merton acknowledges that at this point in his life he found Dante's journey through purgatory interesting and informative yet in no way connected with his own life.

Speaking of his classes on Dante he says,

> And now in the Christian Lent, which I was observing
> without merit and without reason, for the sake of a
> sport which I had grown to detest because I was so
> unsuccessful in it, we were climbing from circle to
> circle of Purgatory.... [I]t seems to me that I was
> armored and locked within my own defectible and
> blinded self by seven layers of...the capital sins which
> only the fires of Purgatory or of Divine Love (they are
> about the same) can burn away.[82]

At this point Dante's purgatory is little more for Merton
than a part of the content of a literature course. In Dante's
purgatory those who dwell there are described "Upon a
burning mountain souls in fire, yet content in fire."[83] They
are "in fire" because they endure separation from God as
they are being purified. They are "content" because they
possess God's love but not yet in the fullness for which they
are destined.

Merton sensed that the soul's journey up the mountain
of purgatory is an apt image for describing one's own
personal journey through life on this earth. He makes the
image of the ongoing climbing of the mountain of
purgatory a way of describing his own life story.

Some years later after his conversion and Baptism
Merton has linked the imagery of Dante's purgatory with
his own life as he struggles to decide how he should spend
his life, "I was about to set foot on the shore at the foot of
the high, seven circled mountain of a Purgatory steeper
and more arduous than I was able to imagine, and I was not
at all aware of the climbing I was about to have to do."[84]

In explaining his personal struggle he says, "All that

---

[82] Thomas Merton, *The Seven Storey Mountain*, p. 122.

[83] Dante Alighieri, *The Inferno*, trans. John Ciardi (New York, N.Y.: The New
American Library, Inc., 1954), p. 31.

[84] Merton, *The Seven Storey Mountain*, p. 221.

occupied me now was the immediate practical problem of getting up my hill with this terrific burden I had on my shoulders, step by step, begging God to drag me along and get me away from my enemies and from those who were trying to destroy me."[85]

At another point in his life he continues to use the image of the mountain but with a difference, "Back in the world I felt like a man that had come down from the rare atmosphere of a very high mountain."[86] Instead of the ongoing climbing of a mountain, he sees himself as one who has been to the mountaintop and has now returned to "the valley" of day-by-day living.

Merton made the imagery of the mountain personal to himself as a way of explaining to himself and to others something of his personal journey. He made the imagery of Dante's seven storey mountain of purgatory so fully his own that he entitled his life story, up to the time he enters a Trappist monastery, *The Seven Storey Mountain*.

The Mountain: Martin Luther King

Martin Luther King was immersed in the Bible. He found a special kinship with the person of Moses. First, review some of the highlights of Moses' life: He is called by God to lead a people out of the land of slavery to a land of freedom. In the course of that forty-year journey Moses goes up to Mount Sinai, undergoes a transforming religious experience and brings back to the people the good news that God's relationship with them is one of love and commitment.

Near the end of his life Moses is aware that it's his

[85] Merton, *The Seven Storey Mountain*, p. 301.
[86] Merton, *The Seven Storey Mountain*, p. 332.

mission to bring the people close to a promised land. He is also aware that he will not live to see them arrive there. Just before Moses' death, God leads him to the top of another mountain, Mount Nebo, from which he sees the promised land, but he knows that he will not live to enter it.

King found in Moses a guide, an example and an inspiration for his own life. In the last talk he gave on the night before his death in Memphis, he reveals the extent to which the life of Moses and the imagery of the mountain have been incorporated into his own life. His concluding words were these,

> I don't know what will happen now.... But it doesn't matter with me now. Because I've been to the mountaintop. And I don't mind. Like anybody, I would like to live a long life. Longevity has its place. But I'm not concerned about that now. I just want to do God's will. And He's allowed me to go up to the mountain. And I've looked over. And I've seen the promised land. I may not get there with you. But I want you to know tonight, that we, as a people, will get to the promised land. And I'm happy, tonight. I'm not worried about anything. I'm not fearing any man. Mine eyes have seen the glory of the coming of the Lord.[87]

In the lives of Thomas Merton and Martin Luther King we see examples of each of them using the mountain image in a personal way. Each made that image his own. The image became for each of them a way of envisioning and coming to terms with his personal past, present and future.

Merton visualized his personal past as an ongoing climbing of the mountain of purgatory in imitation of Dante. King visualized his personal past as both an ascent to and a

[87] Martin Luther King, Jr., *A Testament of Hope: The Essential Writings of Martin Luther King, Jr.*, ed. J.M. Washington (San Francisco: Harper and Row, Publishers, 1986), p. 286.

return from a mountain in imitation of Moses.

The image of the mountain also became for each a way of interpreting the meaning of his life at the present moment. For Merton the cleansing and purifying involved in climbing the mountain of purgatory continues at the present moment. Climbing the mountain of purgatory becomes a way of interpreting the mixture of love and pain occurring in his life at the present.

For King his trip to the mountain is "done" in the sense that he has been to the mountain and has returned. Yet his journey to the mountain continues to exercise an influence upon the present moment in his life. The memory of his journey to the mountain is the cause of his contentment at the present moment.

The image of the mountain also became for each a way of envisioning the future, not by trying to foretell the future but rather by placing himself in a proper relationship with whatever happens in the future.

For Merton climbing the mountain of purgatory is a way of visualizing himself being transformed by God's love in the midst of whatever the future may bring. In a similar way for King there is a sense in which what the future brings doesn't matter. What matters is that he has been to the mountain and that memory will sustain him, no matter what the future brings.

Testing Sacred Moments

You ought not to duck testing the sacred moments in your life. The test consists of asking whether such moments are genuine religious experience or not. Abraham Maslow speaks of the hazards involved in sacred moments, or to use his term, "peak experiences." One "may become simply a selfish person, seeking his own personal salvation, trying to get into 'heaven' even if other people can't, and finally perhaps *using* other people as triggers, as means to his sole end of higher states of consciousness. In a word, he may become not only selfish but also evil."[88]

Sacred moments may be tested in the light of whether they make us more receptive of other people, more capable of being present to others, more capable of listening to others. In religious terms it's the difference between faith and fanaticism. Human beings become fanatical when sacred moments prevent us from listening to others.

One test you can use to verify the sacred moments in your life is found in the conversation of Jesus and Peter after the Resurrection. Jesus has the final word with, "Feed my lambs.... Look after my sheep" (John 21:15-16). Here Jesus gives a standard by which sacred moments in one's life may be tested. Here he gives a standard by which true religious experience is to be distinguished from what is counterfeit, namely, the deepening of one's loving service of other members of the human family.

John Dunne tells a story that illustrates some of the dangers involved in special moments. It is the story of the person who goes to the top of a mountain in search of God only to find that God is not on the mountain. God has gone down from the mountain to the valley where human beings live:

> Consider the following parable. I call it the Parable of the Mountain. Man, let us say, is climbing a mountain. At the top of the mountain, he thinks, is God. Down in the valley are the cares and concerns of human life, all the troubles of love and war. By climbing the

[88] Abraham H. Maslow, *Religions, Values, and Peak Experiences* (New York, N.Y.: Viking Press, 1970), pp. viii and ix.

mountain and reaching the top man hopes to escape
from all these miseries. God, on the other hand, is
coming down the mountain, let us say, his desire
being to plunge himself into the very things that man
wishes to escape. Man's desire is to be God, God's is
to be man. God and man pass one another going in
opposite directions. When man reaches the top of the
mountain he is going to find nothing. God is not
there. Let us suppose that man does reach the top and
does make this discovery. Or suppose that he passes
God on the way, or finds God's tracks leading
downwards, or hears a rumor that God is descending
the mountain. One way or another man learns that
climbing was a mistake and that what he seeks is to
be found only by going down into the valley. He turns
around, therefore, and starts going down the
mountain. He sets his face towards love and war,
where before he had turned his back on them.[89]

One interpretation of the story is that the story of God
and yourself is only part of the story. The story of your
search for God is incomplete unless it also includes your
relationship with members of the human family. The
sacred moments in your life are not a possession to be
clung to but rather a gift to be received and in some way
shared. The goal of the Christian life is not the pursuit of
extraordinary experience but rather the loving service of
others.

Questions for Reflection and Discussion

1) Which use of the mountain image seems to fit your life
   better: the ongoing climbing of a mountain or the ascent
   of a mountain and the return to the valley?

2) Are there sacred moments in your life of which it can be

[89] Dunne, *The Way of All the Earth*, p. 14.

said: Everything before them may be seen as a preparation for them; everything afterward may be seen as flowing from them?

3) In what sense can you speak of the present moment as a sacred moment?

4) In the light of Jesus' Resurrection Peter better understood his own experience of beholding Jesus' transfiguration some time before. What are some examples in your life in which the memory of a past experience moves/motivates you more now than the original experience did at the time it happened?

5) For Thomas Merton and Martin Luther King the image of the mountain was personal. Each made it his own. What image or images are personal to you? What ones have you made your own?

Exercise

This exercise involves your memory and your imagination. You will be visualizing someone from your life, living or deceased. Perhaps someone in your life has died and you feel you really didn't have a chance to say good-bye or a chance to speak your mind. Perhaps you are harboring resentment toward someone living and for any number of reasons you will not be in a situation to tell this person face to face what's bothering you.

In either case you run the risk of becoming stuck in your personal past. You have some unfinished business to attend to so that your personal journey can continue on track.

This exercise may be called the empty chair exercise. In

the privacy of a room, pick an empty chair. Open the door and visualize the person with whom you're going to talk standing there. Visualize this person as distinctly as you can. Welcome this person to the room. Offer this person the empty chair.

You take a seat and, maintaining eye contact with the person you're visualizing, you begin in this or a similar fashion, "There are some things I need to tell you." Then you start telling this person what you're feeling about him or her.

Say the words aloud. If there are moments of silence, that's OK. There's no special hurry. The words you say aloud may lead to the rising of more feelings and more words.

When without hurrying you reach the point at which you are content you have said all that needs to be said, you thank the person for coming. You say this conversation was an important moment to enable the two of you to have a better relationship from this point on.

**Suggestions for Further Study,
Reflection and Exploration**

1) *The Seven Storey Mountain* (New York: Harcourt Brace Jovanovich, 1948) is Thomas Merton's autobiography up to the time of his taking solemn vows at the Trappist monastery in Gethsemane, Kentucky.

2) The title, *The Seven Storey Mountain*, is a reference to Dante's seven storey mountain of purgatory in *The Divine Comedy*. It consists of three books as the poet travels through hell, purgatory and heaven. Dante's *Purgatorio* (New York, N.Y.: The New American Library,

1964) describes the poet's journey up the seven storey mountain of purgatory.

3) *Moments to Remember: Collected by Candida Lund* (Chicago: Thomas More Press, 1980) consists of descriptions of special moments in the lives of more than fifty women from Helen Keller to Golda Meir. Each description begins with a summary of the woman's life, followed by the woman's personal narrative of a special moment(s) in her life. Also included are fictional heroines such as Nora in Henrik Ibsen's play, *A Doll's House* and Thomas Hardy's *Tess of the D'Urbervilles*.

Chapter Seven

Imagining the Present

Your Life Is a Walk Down a Road

One way of picturing to yourself both yourself and the life you live is to picture a pathway or road. The pathway or road can be entitled "My Life." Picture yourself walking on that road. No matter what this day brings, the situations you face, the people you meet, the difficulties you may encounter, all of them can be seen as a part of this picture you've imagined for yourself, namely, of you walking through your life today.

Picturing your life as a walk down a road means a number of things to you: It means you're moving, you have a goal or purpose; it means you're living your life at your own pace and in your own way—you are neither being pushed down the road nor in Carl Jung's words, being "dragged along"[90] the road, either by outside forces or by other people. It means you have dignity and you are your own person because you're following your path. It means you relate to other people whom you meet on that path, giving to and receiving from them. These are examples of some of the insights and conclusions you come to regarding yourself when you start with the picture of your

[90] Jung, *Answer to Job*, p. 185.

life as a walk down a road.

When you imagine that God is your companion on your walk through life, you find a religious dimension, an added depth to the picture. The Psalms provide examples of the picture of God as your companion on your walk, "...wide room you make for my steps under me, my feet have never faltered.... I need only say, 'I am slipping,' and your love, Yahweh, immediately supports me;..." (Psalms 18:36; 93:18).

A variation of the image of God as your companion is to imagine God as a light that illumines your path. As the psalmist says, "...my God lights up my darkness;.... Now your word is a lamp to my feet, a light on my path" (Psalms 18:28, 119:105).

This imagery is expressed in John Henry Newman's "Lead Kindly Light": "Lead, kindly Light,... lead Thou me on. The night is dark and I am far from home. Lead Thou me on. Keep Thou my feet; I do not ask to see the distant scene—one step enough for me."[91]

In contrast, you may also imagine God as darkness or God as present with you in the midst of darkness. The image in this instance is of no clear path in front of you or of a path completely covered in darkness. Edith Stein quotes St. John of the Cross and his use of the image of "no road": "Let us live here on earth as pilgrims...exiles and orphans, in dryness, without a road or anything else, but hoping all things."[92]

Thomas Merton speaks to God, imagined as hidden in darkness, in this prayer,

> My Lord God, I have no idea where I am going. I do

---

[91] John Henry Newman, *Lead Kindly Light*, ed. R.D. Lumb (Westminster: Newman Press, 1958), p. 8.

[92] Edith Stein, *The Science of the Cross* (Chicago, Ill.: Henry Regnery Co., 1960), pp. 211-212.

not see the road ahead of me. I cannot know for
certain where it will end. Nor do I really know myself,
and the fact that I think I am following your will does
not mean that I am actually doing so. But I believe
that the desire to please you does in fact please you.
And I hope I have that desire in all that I am doing. I
hope that I will never do anything apart from that
desire. And I know that if I do this you will lead me by
the right road, though I may know nothing about it.
Therefore I will trust you always though I may seem
to be lost and in the shadow of death. I will not fear,
for you are ever with me, and you will never leave me
to face my perils alone.[93]

A Walk With Others and Alone

When you imagine that Jesus is your companion (or the
one you are walking toward), you find a Christian
dimension in the picture of your life as a walk down a road.
You may also picture other companions with you on the
walk, people you care for, those who are entrusted to you,
those to whom you are entrusted, living and deceased.

Theologians make a distinction between mediated
experience and unmediated experience. Mediated
experience refers to the experience of a mediator between
you and God. "Mediator" used here means someone or
something that stands between God and you or someone
who stands with you before God.

By contrast unmediated experience is the experience of
being alone with God. It is unmediated in the sense that
there is in this experience no mediator—that is, nothing or
no one between you and God.

Biblical examples of the unmediated experience of God
include Jacob, " '...I have seen God face to face...and I have

[93] Thomas Merton, *Thoughts in Solitude* (New York, N.Y.: Farrar, Straus and
Giroux, 1976), p. 83.

survived' " (Genesis 32:31) and Moses, "Since then, never has there been such a prophet in Israel as Moses, the man Yahweh knew face to face" (Deuteronomy 34:10).

Moses' experience of God was unmediated whereas the experience of God of those with him was mediated with Moses as the mediator, "Whenever he went into Yahweh's presence to speak with him, Moses would remove the veil until he came out again. And when he came out, he would tell the sons of Israel what he had been ordered to pass on to them, and the sons of Israel would see the face of Moses radiant" (Exodus 34:34-35).

The distinction between the mediated and the unmediated experience of God may be illustrated in God's calling the prophets Jeremiah and Isaiah. Jeremiah describes the unmediated experience of God; Isaiah the mediated experience of God.

Of Jeremiah, we read,

> The word of Yahweh was addressed to me, saying,
> "Before I formed you in the womb I knew you;
> before you came to birth I consecrated you;
> I have appointed you as prophet to the nations."
> I said, "Ah, Lord Yahweh; look, I do not know how to speak: I am a child!"
> But Yahweh replied, "Do not say, 'I am a child.'
> Go now to those to whom I send you"....
> Then Yahweh put out his hand and touched my mouth and said to me:
> "There! I am putting my words into your mouth."
> (Jeremiah 1:4-9)

What Jeremiah describes is a one-on-one conversation between God and him, similar to a conversation between friends in which one is asking the other to do something about which the other has misgivings—God's invitation, Jeremiah's expression of fears and hesitations, God's assurance that Jeremiah will be protected. No others are involved in this meeting.

Jeremiah's unmediated experience of God stands in contrast to the mediated experience of God of the prophet Isaiah, "...I saw the Lord Yahweh seated on a high throne;... above him stood seraphs..." (Isaiah 6:1). Isaiah sees not only God but also angels with him,

> I said:
> "What a wretched state I am in! I am lost,
> for I am a man of unclean lips...
> and my eyes have looked at the King, Yahweh Sabaoth."
> Then one of the seraphs flew to me, holding in his hand a live coal.... With this he touched my mouth and said:
> "See now, this has touched your lips,
> your sin is taken away..."
> Then I heard the voice of the Lord saying:
> "Whom shall I send? Who will be our messenger?"
> "I answered, "Here I am. Send me." (Isaiah 6:5-9)

The conversation between God and Isaiah takes place in the presence of others, namely, the angels. One of the angels helps change Isaiah from one who at the outset describes himself as "lost" to one who says in response to God's invitation, "send me." Isaiah's experience of God is mediated by the presence of the group of angels and in particular by the angel who helps transform him.

Psalm 23 offers us an example of the unmediated experience of God,

> Yahweh is my shepherd,
>   I lack nothing.
> In meadows of green grass he let me lie.
> To the waters of repose he leads me;
>   there he revives my soul.
> He guides me by paths of virtue
>   for the sake of his name.
> Though I pass through a gloomy valley,

> I fear no harm;
> beside me your rod and your staff
>   are there, to hearten me. (Psalm 23:1-4)

The loving presence of God is expressed and experienced in the form of guidance, protection from harm and without the mediation of others.

By way of contrast Psalm 91 offers us an example of the mediated experience of God,

> ...he will put you in his angels' charge
> to guard you wherever you go.
> They will support you on their hands
> in case you hurt your foot against a stone;....
> (Psalm 91:11, 12)

The loving presence of God is expressed and experienced in the form of guidance, protection from harm and with the mediation of others, the angels.

Carl Jung offers a contemporary expression of the unmediated experience of God when he says, "The spiritual adventure of our time is the exposure of human consciousness to the unknown and unknowable."[94] In Jung's description you stand alone before the Mystery we call God:

> From the beginning I had a sense of destiny, as though my life was assigned to me by fate and had to be fulfilled. This gave me an inner security, and, though I could never prove it to myself, it proved itself to me. *I* did not have this certainty: *it* had me. Nobody could rob me of the conviction that it was enjoined upon me to do what God wanted and not what I wanted. That gave me the strength to go my own way. Often I had the feeling that in all decisive matters I was no longer among men, but was alone with God. And when I was "there," where I was no longer alone, I was outside time; I belonged to the centuries; and

---

[94] Carl G. Jung, *Psychology and Religion: West and East*, trans. R.F.C. Hull (New York, N.Y.: Pantheon Books, 1958), p. 105.

> He who then gave answer was He who had always
> been, who had been before my birth. He who always
> is was there. These talks with the "Other" were my
> profoundest experiences: on the one hand a bloody
> struggle, on the other supreme ecstasy.[95]

Walking through your life upright as well as the unmediated experience of God, namely, walking alone with God, is expressed in the words of the song:

> When you walk through a storm,
> hold your head up high
> And don't be afraid of the dark,
> At the end of the storm is a golden sky
> And the sweet silver song of a lark.
> Walk on through the wind,
> Walk on through the rain,
> Tho' your dreams be tossed and blown
> Walk on, walk on, with hope in your heart,
> And you'll never walk alone,
> You'll never walk alone![96]

In contrast to Jung, John Dunne speaks of the spiritual adventure of passing over to the lives of other people through sympathetic understanding and coming back to our own life enriched by this process,

> The holy man of our time, it seems, is not a figure like
> Gotama or Jesus or Mohammed, a man who could
> found a world religion, but a figure like Gandhi, a man
> who passes over by sympathetic understanding from
> his own religion to other religions and comes back
> with new insight to his own. Passing over and coming
> back, it seems, is the spiritual adventure of our time.[97]

Dunne's spiritual adventure of passing over and coming back is an example of mediated experience. Your journey to

---

[95] Jung, *Memories, Dreams, Reflections*, p. 48.
[96] Rodgers and Hammerstein, *Carousel* (New York, N.Y.: RCA Victor Dynagroove Recording, 1965).
[97] Dunne, *The Way of All the Earth*, p. ix.

God is mediated by the lives of others who have entered your life and whose lives you have entered. In some way they are with you in your relationship with God.

Christianity may be described as a religion of the mediated experience of God, in accord with the words of St. Paul, "For there is only one God, and there is only one mediator between God and mankind, himself a man, Christ Jesus, who sacrificed himself as a ransom for them all" (1 Timothy 2:5-6). When you experience your relationship with Jesus as one of companionship with him in relation to the God he called "Abba," "Father," your experience is mediated experience. Jesus is your mediator, your companion in your walk toward God.

We can distinguish among some Christian faith groups a tendency toward the unmediated experience of God. We can distinguish among other Christian faith groups a tendency toward the mediated experience of God.

Traditional Catholic religious experience tends to be characterized more by mediated experience than by unmediated. You tend to stand before God with the mediation of saints and things, such as bread, wine, oil, ashes, candles, incense.

The Second Eucharistic Prayer offers a typical expression of mediated experience,

> ...make us worthy to share eternal life
> with Mary, the virgin Mother of God,
> with the apostles, and with all the saints
> who have done Your will throughout the ages.
> May we praise you *in union with them*,
> and give you glory
> through your Son, Jesus Christ.[98]

Traditional Protestant religious experience tends to be

[98] English translation of the *Roman Missal* (Washington, D.C.: International Commission on English in the Liturgy, 1973).

characterized more by unmediated experience than by mediated experience. You tend to stand alone before God without the mediation of saints.

This contrast between the Catholic and the Protestant traditions is illustrated by the approach of a theologian from each tradition. Catholic theologian Charles Curran cites Protestant theologian Karl Barth who "said that his greatest problem with Roman Catholicism was its 'and.' There is no doubt that the 'and' has traditionally characterized Catholic self-understanding—Scripture *and* tradition, faith *and* reason, divine *and* human, grace *and* nature, Jesus *and* the church, and Mary *and* the saints. In my perspective it is precisely the Catholic 'and' which is very satisfying."[99]

The contrast is not an attempt to label religious faith groups. Nor is it to say that one kind of experience is better than the other. It is to say, however, that the religious experience of members of a particular religious faith group will tend more toward one than the other—either mediated or unmediated religious experience.

Dunne develops the thesis that some lives can be looked upon as a search for unmediated experience whereas the lives of others can be looked upon as a search for mediated experience:

> Each of the figures we have just considered solved more or less successfully the problem of despair, some of them, Luther, Bunyan, Wesley, and Kierkegaard, within the situation of unmediated existence, and some of them, Erasmus, Pascal, Liguori, and Newman, by recourse to mediation in some form.[100]

[99] Charles E. Curran, *Faithful Dissent* (Kansas City, Mo.: Sheed and Ward, 1986), p. 76.
[100] Dunne, *A Search for God in Time and Memory*, p. 92.

Dunne suggests that the spiritual adventure of our time consists of both unmediated experience as expressed by Carl Jung and mediated experience in the sense of passing over to the lives of others and returning enriched to one's own. You do not have to choose between mediated and unmediated experience. Each can be incorporated into your life.

A Stranger on the Road

When you look upon your life as a walk down a road, you can expand the meaning of that image to include not only walking but other kinds of traveling. The themes of the journey and the one who travels are often found in Scripture.

The tent dweller is an image often used in Scripture to portray both travel and traveler. The image suggests one whose abode is not permanent, one whose way of life includes frequent movement from place to place. The tent dweller's story is a mirror that reflects your own life as a walk. You find something of yourself in the tent dweller. The tent dweller's story in some way becomes your story.

The story of Abraham is the story of one who is on the move. "Yahweh said to Abram, 'Leave your country, your family and your father's house, for the land I will show you'" (Genesis 12:1). The author of the Letter to the Hebrews tells us more about Abraham the traveler, "It was by faith that Abraham obeyed the call to *set out* for a country that was the inheritance given to him and his descendants, and that *he set out* without knowing where he was going. By faith he arrived, *as a foreigner*, in the Promised Land, and lived there as if in a strange country, with Isaac and Jacob, who were heirs with him of the same promise. They lived there in tents while he looked forward to a city founded, designed and built by God" (Hebrews 11:8-9).

Abraham's vocation not only involved traveling from one place to another but also involved traveling and dwelling in a foreign country. It is one thing to travel and dwell in familiar places where one feels at home; it is quite another thing to travel and live on foreign soil as not only a traveler but a stranger as well.

Abraham's story reminds you that God's call will involve you in being a stranger, a stranger to much that this world holds dear, a stranger who is not quite at home now in this world. Theologians make a distinction between "now" and "not yet." The kingdom of God is happening *now* within you and outside you; at the same time the kingdom of God has *not yet* happened in its fullness and completeness.

There is a tension involved in the awareness, for example, that Christ is our peace now and at the same time peace is something yet to be achieved both within yourself and in the world outside yourself. It is the tension of loving the world God has created, "...and God saw that it was good" (Genesis 1:10), and at the same time resisting and striving to overcome the world of sinful, destructive, dehumanizing influences that exist both within and outside yourself, "...be brave: I have conquered the world" (John 16:33).

This kind of tension means that you are a stranger on the earth. Abraham's story is also your story. Part of your calling consists of not forgetting who and what you are—the traveler, the stranger. The refrain echoes through the Old Testament that not only were you a stranger but also you still are a stranger. Being a stranger is not just a past reality but also a present fact, "Land must not be sold in perpetuity, for the land belongs to me, and to me you are only strangers and guests" (Leviticus 25:23).

If you remember, then your response to the infirm, the poor, the have-nots, those in any way not in the mainstream, those on the fringe will not be that of the insider who shares wealth with those less fortunate. Rather it will be the response of one stranger to another; it will be the response of one who does not have it made in this world to brothers and sisters in need who also do not have it made in this world. If you remember that you are a stranger, then you can hope to respond to the biblical mandate, "Love the stranger then, for you were strangers in the land of Egypt" (Deuteronomy 10:19).

If you remember that you are a stranger and in some way are called to remain a stranger on this earth, you will not look for utopia or perfection on this earth. If you remember that you are a stranger, you may be less inclined to place an enormous weight of expectation on the people in your life to take your strangeness or loneliness away.

To be a stranger in the biblical sense can heighten your awareness of your vocation to make this world less inhuman, less unjust. You do so not in the sense of expecting to create heaven upon earth but rather to help make this world less cruel, less foreign, less strange.

In William Faulkner's novel *Intruder in the Dust*, Gavin Stevens says to his nephew Chick Mallison, "Some things you must always be unable to bear. Some things you must never stop refusing to bear. Injustice and outrage and dishonor and shame. No matter how young you are or how old you have got. Not for kudos and not for cash: your picture in the paper nor money in the bank either. Just refuse to bear them."[101]

It is important that you not be at home in a world of injustice and outrage and dishonor and shame. Some degree of alienation is part of your vocation as a stranger in a cruel world.

Christopher Fry uses the imagery of a walk in relation to the mystery of evil we face,

> Thank God our time is now when wrong
> Comes to face us everywhere,
> Never to leave us till we take
> The longest stride of soul men ever took.[102]

Some months ago Mother Teresa was interviewed by a reporter regarding her work with destitute people around the world. The reporter noted that in spite of all her efforts and the efforts of the religious community she founded, poverty is apparently as much in evidence now as it was before she started. Her reply was, "God does not ask us to be successful. He asks us to be faithful." So too with ourselves God does not ask that we always succeed. He does ask that we be faithful, faithful to the people, to the gifts and to the opportunities that are placed in our hands.

Imagining Your Relationship With Those in Need: Us and Them

At the Last Supper Jesus says, "You will all lose faith in me this night" (Matthew 26:31). Peter is quick to deny Jesus' words, "Though all lose faith in you, I will never lose faith" (Matthew 26:33). Jesus replies, "I tell you solemnly,

[101] William Faulkner, *Intruder in the Dust* (New York, N.Y.: Random House, Inc., 1948), p. 206.
[102] Christopher Fry, "A Sleep of Prisoners," *Three Plays* (New York, N.Y.: Oxford University Press, 1968), p. 209.

this very night, before the cock crows, you will have disowned me three times" (Matthew 26:34).

Peter refuses to acknowledge that the possible failure of the others might say something about his possible failure. He refuses to see anything of himself in the others. The fact that they could fail does not say anything to him about himself. Peter is speaking from an attitude that may be described as an "us and them" attitude: There are two groups of people in the world, those who would never betray Jesus, the group known as "us," and the group of those who might betray Jesus, the group known as "them."

Peter places himself with the "us"; he places the other disciples with the "them." However, Peter was to learn in a few hours from painful, personal experience that an attitude that draws a line between "us and them" is a false and self-deceiving attitude.

Jesus reveals the folly of this attitude in the story of the Pharisee and the publican. The Pharisee sees himself as part of "us"—the "in" group. He thanks God he is one of the elite, one of the inner circle. He places the publican with "them"—the "out" group, those either separated from God or at least less human and less moral because he is not one of "us."

The publican by contrast acknowledges his distance from God and acknowledges he is a sinner. The publican doesn't divide the world into "us and them" because he finds something of himself in other human beings and something of them in him.

As happens so often in Jesus' parables the tables end up turned. The Pharisee who pictures himself close to God is the one who is distant from him. The publican who pictures Judgment Day, himself distant from God, is the one who is drawing close to him.

The "us and them" attitude is portrayed in Flannery O'Connor's short story, "Revelation." Mrs. Turpin draws a line between "respectable" people and "trash." She has a vision of Judgment Day,

> ...[A] vast horde of souls were rumbling toward heaven. There were whole companies of white-trash, clean for the first time in their lives.... And bringing up the end of the procession was a tribe of people whom she recognized at once as those who, like herself and Claud, had always had a little of everything and the God-given wit to use it right. She leaned forward to observe them closer. They were marching behind the others with great dignity, accountable as they had always been for good order and common sense and respectable behavior. They alone were on key. Yet she could see by their shocked and altered faces that even their virtues were being burned away.[103]

Mrs. Turpin is not surprised to find the "trash" being cleansed of their faults. What stuns her is to find that the "respectable" people are being cleansed of some of their virtues, such as arrogance and self-righteousness.

An "us and them" attitude makes it easy for you to project upon others conflicts within yourself and aspects of yourself that you are not facing. It is easy for you to criticize in others what you do not acknowledge or recognize in yourself.

> This is not to say that M. LeGrandin was anything but sincere when he inveighed against snobs. He could not (from his own knowledge, at least) be aware that he himself was one, since it is only with the passions of others that we are ever really familiar, and what we discover about our own can only be learned from them.[104]

[103] Flannery O'Connor, "Revelation," *The Complete Stories* (New York, N.Y.: Farrar, Straus and Giroux, 1971), p. 508.
[104] Proust, Vol. I, p. 140.

Carl Jung notes, "Everything that irritates us about others can lead us to an understanding of ourselves." [105]

There is a group of people that receives great attention in both the Old and New Testament, a group described in various ways as the poor, the sorrowing, the lowly, the humble, the foolish, the little ones. Before you try to understand what Scripture says about the poor, you first need to be aware of the "us and them" attitude, an attitude which in this case would divide the human family into two groups—"them" referring to the poor, and "us" referring to those who are not poor. Then you need to move away from that attitude by seeing that it's a quite inadequate way of describing your relationship with other human beings.

You begin by acknowledging to yourself that the poor do not exist only outside yourself. You begin by acknowledging to yourself that you are one of the poor. You can gain a glimpse into your poverty by reminding yourself, for example, that every breath you draw is miraculous, as miraculous as the first breath you ever drew. What would you be, what would you have without the constant, sustaining Presence of the Living Mystery we call God? What would you be? You would be nothing. How can you be poorer than that?

St. Paul asks the question in this way, "What do you have that was not given to you? And if it was given, how can you boast as though it were not?" (1 Corinthians 4:7). If you insist upon dividing the world into groups, you might better make a distinction between those who acknowledge their poverty and emptiness before God and those who don't.

In addition to being one of the poor, you are also one of the rich. You are rich, first of all, with the gift of human life, a gift you tend to take so much for granted, a gift which is

[105] Jung, *Memories, Dreams, Reflections*, p. 247.

the basis of so many other gifts. You are rich in gifts, rich in talents, rich in opportunities.

Approach the written word of God with the awareness that you are both one of the poor and one of the rich. Nowhere do the standards of Jesus clash more with those of the world than when the subject is the rich and the poor, the weak and the powerful, the wise and the foolish. Mary, the mother of Jesus, summarizes it in her prayer: "My soul proclaims the greatness of the Lord and my spirit *exults in God my savior;.... He has pulled down princes* from their thrones *and exalted the lowly. The hungry he has filled with good things*, the rich sent empty away" (Luke 1:47-53).

When Mary declares that God has exalted the lowly, you are encouraged because you are one of the poor. At the same time Mary's words challenge the rich and powerful; her words challenge you because you are also one of the rich. You acknowledge your riches by trying to develop and use the gifts that have been given to you. In this way the saying becomes true: "The glory of God *is* human development. The glory of God *is* human growth."

You acknowledge your riches by trying to live in a way that makes the world a little less unjust, a little less inhuman. At the same time you acknowledge your poverty by remaining mindful of the Source of your gifts, of all that you are and all that you have—"...cut off from me you can do nothing" (John 15:5).

Questions for Reflection and Discussion

1) In what ways do you picture or imagine God as your companion?

2) Which do you relate to more easily: the unmediated experience of God, as illustrated in Jeremiah, or the mediated experience of God, as illustrated in Isaiah? Why?

3) What are some examples from your life of the unmediated experience of God?

4) What are some examples from your life of the mediated experience of God?

5) What are some examples from your life to illustrate the tension of both loving the world and also resisting the world?

6) How can you try to live out the calling of the stranger to help make this world less inhuman?

7) Do you agree with Jung's statement that everything that irritates us about others can lead us to an understanding of ourselves? Give examples.

8) What are some examples from your life of needing to resist the "us and them" attitude?

9) What are some examples that illustrate that you are one of the poor, one of the rich?

Exercise

This exercise begins with the image of your life as a walk down a road. Your walk through life today is one in which your walk is not confined in space.

Your walk today will bring you into contact with absent loved ones, living or deceased. You visualize an absent loved one. In your visualization you surround this person with light. The light is God's love and your love. You speak to this person as you hold on to the visualizing you're doing.

At other times words may not be necessary or helpful. As you keep visualizing the absent loved one, there is a shared presence that goes on between you and the other. Words may not be needed. Shared presence is enough.

Prayer may take the simple form of a conversation with the absent loved one. In conversation words have a place. In conversation silence and listening will at times be more important. In this way there is no place on God's earth or beyond that is beyond your walking through in your imagination.

Suggestions for Further Study, Reflection and Exploration

1) The poor and the oppressed are the subjects of *A Theology of Liberation: History, Politics and Salvation*, by Gustavo Gutierrez (Maryknoll, N.Y.: Orbis Books, 1971), described by some as the Magna Carta of liberation theology. Gutierrez develops the term "liberation" as a better term than "development" to describe the struggle for a more just society in which people live with dignity.

2) Thomas Merton's *Conjectures of a Guilty Bystander* (Garden City, N.Y.: Doubleday and Co., Inc., 1968) contains his personal reflections and meditations on a wide range of contemporary issues.

3) *Therese* (Springfield, Ill.: Templegate, 1979) is a biography of St. Therese of Lisieux by Dorothy Day. At first glance Dorothy Day, political activist, and Therese of Lisieux, Carmelite nun, may seem to be worlds apart. Not so, as this book reveals. Dorothy discovers that her concern for the poor and the oppressed and Therese's concern for the "little people" who would follow her "little way" of spiritual childhood are similar pathways.

Chapter Eight

Imagining Your Future

Your Life is a Walk to the Center of a Circle

John Dunne adds another imaginative dimension to the picture of your life as a walk—as a walk from a point on the circumference of a circle to its center:

> Imagine all…standing around the circumference of an immense circle. There are an infinity of points on the circle and each man stands at a different point. There is also a center. The task of each man, let us say, is to go from the circumference to the center. What situates a man on the circumference is the partiality of his self; what stands at the center would be the integral self.[106]

Your life pictured as a journey from the circumference of a circle to its center reminds you that your path to the center is personal to you. No one else can take this journey for you. At the same time you are related to many others while you make your personal journey. Yet no matter how close the bonds of friendship and love may be between you and the others in your life, you are called to make your personal journey from the circumference to the center just as each of them is called to make a personal journey.

Pierre Teilhard de Chardin writes, "Obviously I cannot

---

[106] Dunne, *A Search for God in Time and Memory*, p. 119.

abandon my own personal search—that would involve me in an interior catastrophe to my most cherished vocation."[107]

In similar ways, religion is personal, private and individual. This is not to say religion is limited to these dimensions, nor is it to deny or minimize the fact that religion involves relatedness with others and with the world in which we live. It is to say, however, that one can quite properly speak of *my* religious belief and personal religion. In the words of John Steinbeck, "It isn't true that there's a community of light, a bonfire of the world. Everyone carries his own, his lonely own."[108]

Indeed, in the book of Exodus God says to Moses, "I am the God of your father,...the God of Abraham, the God of Isaac and the God of Jacob" (Exodus 3:6). What is described is not a vague divinity or abstraction but rather a God whose relationship with human beings is so intimate that he may be described as God in terms of those human beings, i.e., the God of Abraham or the God of Isaac. In a similar way as we look at personalities in history we may speak, for example, of the God of Augustine, the God of Thomas Aquinas or the God of Teresa of Avila.

To affirm that religion is personal is part of your task in trying to strike a balance between your relationship with yourself and others. That balance can be visualized by the picture of the individual pathways leading to the center of the circle. As John Dunne expresses it, "What is more, I see all the radial paths converging, that the further we go...the closer we come to each other. To the extent that I follow my personal path to the center, I come closer to God and

[107] Pierre Teilhard de Chardin, *The Divine Milieu* (New York, N.Y.: Harper and Row, Publishers, 1960), p. 39.
[108] John Steinbeck, *The Winter of Our Discontent*, (New York, N.Y.: Viking Press, 1961), p. 311.

closer to the people in my life."[109]

The statement "I am different from everyone else" is a statement of the story of your uniqueness. The statement "I am the same as everyone else" is a statement of the story of your commonness, your universality, what you share with everyone else. Perhaps the difference between these two statements is not as great as first appears. Perhaps as I pursue my uniqueness and you pursue your uniqueness, we are coming closer to what is shared by each of us.

The Path Chosen: You Are Not Alone on Your Walk to the Center

While the story of your walk is important and necessary, it is not the whole story. While the path you pursue continues to be your path, another part of the story is that you are not alone as you pursue your path.

> One night a man had a dream. He dreamed he was walking along the beach with the Lord. Across the sky flashed scenes from his life. For each scene he noticed two sets of footprints in the sand, one belonging to him and the other to the Lord.

> When the last scene of his life flashed before him, he looked back at the footprints in the sand. He noticed that many times along the path of his life there was only one set of footprints. He also noticed that it happened at the very lowest and saddest times of his life.

> This really bothered him and he questioned the Lord about it. "Lord, you said that once I decided to follow you, you'd walk with me all the way. But I have noticed that during the most troublesome times of my life, there is only one set of footprints. I don't understand why when I needed you most, you would leave."

[109] Dunne, *A Search for God in Time and Memory*, p. 104.

The Lord replied, "My precious, precious child. I love you and I would never leave you. During your times of trial and suffering, when you see only one set of footprints, it was then that I carried you."

Choosing Your Path: The Path Chosen for You

You may wonder if your present path is right for you. Is it leading you closer to or farther away from the center? In the midst of the questions asked, the Psalms reassure you of the presence of one who is with you, "[Y]ou have rescued me from Death to walk in the presence of God in the light of the living..." (Psalm 56:13).

You are confident that you will be shown the path to follow: "[Y]ou will reveal the path to life to me,.... Everyone who fears Yahweh will be taught the course a man should choose" (Psalm 16:11; 25:12).

The image of God as your companion on your walk births expressions of prayer such as, "You will reveal the path of life to me.... [T]each me your paths.... [L]ead me in the path of integrity.... Direct my steps as you have promised,..." (Psalms 16:11; 25:4; 27:11; 119:133).

The dangers you face are less threatening as you realize that "your path" is becoming more a path upon which you are being led in safety: "My eyes are always on Yahweh, for he releases my feet from the net.... All Yahweh's paths are love and truth..." (Psalm 25:15, 10).

Jesus images God as your shepherd guiding you and applies this image of the Good Shepherd to himself. This Good Shepherd not only guides his disciples on their path but walks ahead of them on the path to lead them:

> ...[T]he sheep hear his voice, one by one he calls his own sheep and leads them out. When he has brought

out his flock, he goes ahead of them, and the sheep follow him because they know his voice.... I am the good shepherd.... The sheep that belong to me listen to my voice; I know them and they follow Me." (John 10:3-4, 11, 27)

Jesus gives us yet another image of following him on a path, the image of one who has carried a cross, inviting his followers to follow him in the same way, "If anyone wants to be a follower of mine, let him renounce himself and take up his cross and follow Me" (Matthew 16:24).

St. Peter expands upon the image of following in his footsteps, "The merit, in the sight of God, is in bearing it patiently when you are punished after doing your duty.... This, in fact, is what you were called to do, because Christ suffered for you and left an example for you to follow the way he took" (1 Peter 2:20, 21).

You find that following your path leads to following the path upon which someone else is leading you. Choosing your path leads to following the path chosen for you, as expressed by Dag Hammarskjöld:

Weep
If you can,
Weep,
But do not complain.
The way chose you—
And you must be thankful.[110]

As John Dunne expresses it, "The path I devise for myself vanishes but the path meant for me opens before me."[111]

---

[110] Dag Hammarskjöld, *Markings* (New York, N.Y.: Alfred A. Knopf, Inc., 1964), p. 213.
[111] Dunne, *A Search for God in Time and Memory*, p. 129.

Teilhard de Chardin and 'The Center'

Teilhard de Chardin gives attention to the "center" toward which your path and everyone's path is converging. He speaks of the final point of the evolutionary process as "a centre, possessing the qualities of a centre. Now what is the only way in which a centre can be formed and sustained as such? Is it by breaking down the lower centres which fall under its governance? Indeed it is not—it is by strengthening them in its own image."[112]

In addition to speaking of God as the center of a circle toward which we are moving, Teilhard de Chardin also speaks of combining two impulses or two kinds of faith, faith in the God ahead of us and faith in the God above us. He illustrates the two with a diagram,

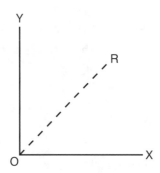

Diagram illustrating the conflict between the two kinds of faith:

OY: Christian faith, aspiring Upward, in a personal transcendency, toward the Highest.

OX: Human faith, driving forward to the ultra-human.

---

[112] Pierre Teilhard de Chardin, *Christianity and Evolution*, trans. René Hague (New York, N.Y.: Harcourt Brace Jovanovich, Inc., 1969), p. 117.

OR: Christian faith "rectified" or "made explicit,"
reconciling the two: salvation (outlet) at once Upward
and Forward in a Christ Who is both Saviour and
Mover.[113]

Teilhard de Chardin gives us an interpretation of the
sign of the cross that includes these two kinds of faith, "I
feel drawn to and satisfied by a Cross in which the two
components of the future are synthesized: the transcendent
and the ultra-human;...the Above and the Ahead."[114]

Teilhard de Chardin expands upon the necessity of
uniting these two kinds of faith, "The supernaturalizing
Christian 'Upward' is incorporated (not immersed) in the
human 'Forward'.... It is because the total Unity of which
we dream still seems to beckon in two different directions,
toward the zenith and toward the horizon, that we see the
dramatic growth of a whole race of 'spiritual expatriates';
human beings torn between a Marxism whose
depersonalizing effect revolts them and a Christianity so
lukewarm it sickens them."[115]

Teilhard de Chardin uses the growth of research in the
sciences as an example of a future direction in which the
human family is moving. At the same time he speaks of the
need for something more than science if the sciences are to
remain human, "[R]eligion is the soul biologically
necessary for the future of science. Humanity is no longer
imaginable without science. But no more is science
possible without some religion to animate it."[116]

Teilhard de Chardin sees the "Ahead" of science joined
to the "Above" of religion in the lives of those who through

---

[113] Pierre Teilhard de Chardin, *The Future of Man* (New York, N.Y.: Harper
and Row, Publishers, 1964), p. 269.
[114] Teilhard de Chardin, *Christianity and Evolution*, pp. 218-219.
[115] Teilhard de Chardin, *The Future of Man*, p. 268.
[116] Pierre Teilhard de Chardin, *Human Energy* (New York, N.Y.: Harcourt
Brace Jovanovich, Inc., 1962), p. 180.

human labor are thereby involved with Something More, "the seeker who devotes himself, ultimately through love, to the labours of discovery. No longer a worshiper of the world but of something greater than the world, through and beyond the world in progress. Not the proud and cold Titan, but Jacob passionately wrestling with God."[117]

Teilhard de Chardin refers to God as the Center of a circle, God ahead of us and God above us with an image from the Book of Revelation—Omega. Alpha and omega are the first and last letters of the Greek alphabet. In the Book of Revelation God says, "I am the Alpha and Omega, *the First and the Last*, the Beginning and the End" (Revelation 22:13-14). He indicates that this final point Omega must be personal, not something but someone— loving and lovable—and therefore capable of drawing free human beings toward full union,

> The essential core of Christianity, in my view, is certainly none of the humanitarian or moral ideals so dear both to believers and unbelievers; it is to maintain and preserve the primacy of the Personal...and also to bring the world into contact with the supreme person, that is to say, give Him a name.

> Ultimately we must seek the principle of our unification not simply in the contemplation of one and the same truth, not simply in the desire aroused by Something, but in the attraction, common to all, exercised by one and the same Someone.[118]

This final point Omega is the person of Jesus Christ. When Teilhard de Chardin's faith in the person of Jesus is added to his commitment as a scientist, a new vision emerges. The vision might be described as a vision of

[117] Teilhard de Chardin, *Human Energy*, p. 181.
[118] Henri de Lubac, *Teilhard de Chardin: The Man and His Meaning* (New York, N.Y.: The New American Library, Inc., 1964), p. 26.

daylight at the end of the human journey, a vision of daylight at the center of the circle.

Teilhard de Chardin elaborates upon his equating Jesus with Omega:

> The Christ of revelation is quite simply Omega. To demonstrate this fundamental proposition, I need only refer to the long series of Joannine and especially Pauline texts where the physical supremacy of Christ over the universe is affirmed in terms which are magnificent.... They all come down to these two essential affirmations: "In Him all things exist" (Colossians 1:17) and "He it is who fills all things" (Ephesians 4:9) so that "Christ may be all in all." (Colossians 3:11). There we have the very definition of Omega.[119]

You picture your personal path leading you from the circumference of a circle toward Omega at the center. Teilhard de Chardin notes, "I believe that the Messiah whom we await, whom we all without any doubt await, is the universal Christ; that is to say, the Christ of evolution."[120]

Omega reminds us that in our personal journey we are being drawn to and attracted by our loving God who placed us here. Omega reminds us that our God is not only within us but also in front of us, leading us forward. In the words of Rainer Maria Rilke, "Why not think that God is He who will come, that He is the future, the final fruit of a tree whose leaves we are?... Don't you see that whatever happens is a beginning?"[121]

Someone has said that God is a circle whose center is everywhere and whose circumference is nowhere. This

---

[119] Christopher M. Mooney, *Teilhard de Chardin and the Mystery of Christ* (New York, N.Y.: Harper and Row, Publishers, 1966), p. 89.

[120] Teilhard de Chardin, *Christianity and Evolution*, p. 95.

[121] Rainer Maria Rilke, *Letters to a Young Poet* (New York, N.Y.: W.W. Norton and Co., Inc., 1934), p. 49.

description suggests another variation of the image of walking toward God who is the Center of a circle. The variation is that because God is within you, you are already at the center of the circle. You already possess within you the One you are moving toward.

This image is an expression of the tension between what theology calls the "already" and the "not yet." You "already" possess Christ through faith, hope and love. "Christ...lives in me" (Galatians 2:20). At the same time you do not yet possess Christ in His fullness. "No one has ever seen God" (1 John 4:12). You possess within you the one whom you do not yet fully possess. You are sustained on your journey toward Omega by the awareness that at each step of the journey you are in some real but mysterious way already there.

Questions for Reflection and Discussion

1) What are some examples that illustrate your religion is personal and private?

2) What are some examples that illustrate your religion is also more than personal and private?

3) What are some examples in which following your path led to following the path upon which Someone is leading you?

4) Which do you relate to more easily: faith in God above us or faith in God ahead of us?

5) What do you make of Teilhard de Chardin's statement of the growth of "spiritual expatriates" who are turned off both by Marxism and lukewarm Christianity?

6) What personal images are "at work" with you when you think about or imagine your future/the future?

Exercise

This exercise in ways of imagining your future can be described as an "as if" exercise. William James was the founder of what has come to be called the "as if" philosophy. Some say that when James doubted that there was a meaning to life, he proceeded to act "as if" there is a meaning to life. When he wondered whether there's anything to hope for, he proceeded to think and to act "as if" there is something to hope for. In times of difficulty he committed himself, as a technique and as an attitude, to acting "as if" a desirable outcome may be achieved.

Your first "as if" exercise can be a simple one. Choose some moment in the next few days that you really are not looking forward to and would rather skip, anything from a dental appointment to a difficult meeting to a difficult task in which you'd rather not be involved.

Your goal is to prepare for and approach this difficult moment "as if" it's not going to be difficult for you. Even more, your goal is to approach this moment "as if" this moment is going to turn out well for you, well beyond your expectations.

You begin in a quiet moment with a visualization. If you are apprehensive about a meeting next week, you visualize the place of that meeting, the person or persons who will be attending.

You visualize the meeting place and those at the meeting surrounded with light. You visualize yourself proceeding through this meeting, its difficulties and problems being absorbed in the light. In the time prior to the meeting that you find yourself worrying and uptight about this meeting, you bring these images of light to mind. You hold on to the images and by holding them in your mind's eye, you begin to relax and calm down.

When the future moment you've been dreading becomes the present moment, you walk into the meeting carrying those images before your mind's eye. An exercise of this sort does not have as its purpose to change the difficulties you face. What it does is change your relationship with the difficulties you face.

**Suggestions for Further Study,
Reflection and Exploration**

1) *The Future of Man* (New York, N.Y.: Harper and Row, Publishers, 1964) offers a good introduction to the thought of Pierre Teilhard de Chardin.

2) The philosophy of "as if" is described by William James in *The Will to Believe* (New York, N.Y.: Dover, 1956) and *Pragmatism and Other Essays* (New York, N.Y.: Washington Square Press, 1963).

3) *Man of La Mancha* by Dale Wasserman (New York, N.Y.: Dell Publishing Co., Inc., 1966) is a popular rendition of the story of Don Quixote and his friend Sancho as originally told in Miguel de Cervantes' *Don Quixote*. Don Quixote's dreams and visions for the future bring him into conflict with so-called "reality."

Part II

"I and Thou"
The Story
Beyond Self

Chapter Nine

Imagining Love Relationships

"I and Thou"

Up to this point your primary concern has been your relationship with yourself. You have looked upon your life story in different ways as a story of your deeds, a story of your experience and a story of your "self." You have pictured your relationship with yourself through images of walking up a mountain, walking down a road and walking to the center of a circle. Your primary concern has been yourself, or as Martin Buber expresses it, the world of "I."

The world of "I," the world of self, is important and necessary. However, the words of Jesus are a reminder that self is not the whole story, "If any[one] comes to me without hating his father, mother, wife, children, brothers, sisters, yes and his own life too, he cannot be my disciple" (Luke 14:26). We are called not only to live a life of "self" but also to live a life "beyond self."

This story beyond self is what Bernard Lonergan describes as "self-transcendence," "loving and being loved," the going beyond one's self that we call love, "Man achieves authenticity in self-transcendence.

"One can live in a world, have a horizon, just in the

measure that one is not locked up in oneself."[122]

> Being-in-love is of different kinds. There is the love of
> intimacy, of husband and wife, of parents and
> children. There is the love of one's fellow men with its
> fruit in the achievement of human welfare. There is
> the love of God with one's whole heart and whole
> soul, with all one's mind and all one's strength (Mark
> 12:30). It is God's love flooding our hearts through
> the Holy Spirit given to us (Romans 5:5)....

> Such being-in-love has its antecedents, its causes, its
> conditions, its occasions. But once it has blossomed
> forth and as long as it lasts, it takes over. It is the first
> principle. From it flow one's desires and fears, one's
> joys and sorrows, one's discernment of values, one's
> decisions and deeds.[123]

Your primary concern now shifts beyond self to your
relationships with others, picturing those relationships
with images and striving to gain understanding from those
images. Your primary concern will be with the world of
what Buber describes as "thou," the world of "I and Thou."

If your relationship with yourself is a mystery, so also
your relationship with others is as much, if not more, of a
mystery. If the world of "I" is a mystery, the world of "I and
Thou" is as much of a mystery—and more so. Those we
love are a mystery to us. We are a mystery to them.

Love does not clear up the mystery of a loved one. It
heightens and deepens the mystery. Jesus' words to Philip,
"Have I been with you all this time...and you still do not
know me?" (John 14:9) indicate that the painfulness of
mystery and misunderstanding in love relationships began
early in Christianity with Jesus and the Twelve.

> Other people are, as a rule, so immaterial to us that,
> when we have entrusted to any one of them the power

---

[122] Lonergan, *Method in Theology*, p. 104.
[123] Lonergan, *Method in Theology*, p. 105.

to cause so much suffering or happiness to ourselves, that person seems at once to belong to a different universe, is surrounded with poetry, makes of our lives a vast expanse, quick with sensation, on which that person and ourselves are ever more or less in contact....

We understand the characters of people who do not interest us; how can we ever grasp that of a person who is an intimate part of our existence, whom after a little while we no longer distinguish in any way from ourselves?[124]

In Buber's words, "Love is responsibility of an I for a Thou. In this lies the likeness...of all who love, from the smallest to the greatest.... The 'Thou' meets me through grace—it is not found by seeking...the 'Thou' meets me but I step into direct relation with it. Hence the relation means chosen and choosing, suffering and action in one.... All real living is meeting."[125] Edith Stein notes, "All depends on love, for at the end of our life we will be judged by it."[126]

Indwelling

Part of the mystery of love is the mystery that can be described as "indwelling." Those whom you love dwell within you. They are an abiding presence with you. You dwell with those who love you. You are an abiding presence with them. Physical absence does not end the indwelling; it changes it. Death does not end the indwelling; it changes it.

You look to Scripture to gain insight into the mystery of indwelling. What you find there about the relationship of Jesus and his followers may help you to imagine the people

[124] Proust, Vol. I, pp. 257, 955, 956.
[125] Martin Buber, *I and Thou* (New York, N.Y.: Charles Scribner's Sons, 1958), pp. 11, 14, 62.
[126] Stein, *The Science of the Cross*, p. 226.

and the relationships in your life in new and different ways.

Everyone gives special attention to the words of one who is near death and knows it. At such a moment we may presume the person will limit activities to essentials. That is one reason why the Christian mind and heart is drawn in a particular way to the words of Jesus at the Last Supper.

In Chapters 13 through 17 of St. John's Gospel we note how few of Jesus' words at the Last Supper are concerned with telling the apostles what they ought to do or what they ought to avoid, and how many of his words are concerned with the mystery of indwelling. We may also describe it as the mystery of presence— their being present to one another, "being there" for each other, his being present in the midst of them and within them.

He speaks of different kinds of presence which also include varieties of the experience of absence, as when he says, "I shall not be with you much longer.... I am going now to prepare a place for you...so that where I am you may be too.... I will not leave you orphans...I am going away, and shall return.... I am the vine, you are the branches...cut off from me you can do nothing.... I am not in the world any longer, but they are in the world, and I am coming to you.... Father, I want those you have given me to be with me where I am,..." (John 13:33; 14:2-3, 18, 28; 15:5; 17:11, 24).

Jesus' words on the theme of indwelling are quite explicit, "If anyone loves me, he will keep my word, and my Father will love him, and we shall come to him and make our home with him" (John 14:23). In fact, Martin Buber makes the observation that "the Gospel according to John is really the Gospel of pure relation."[127]

Jesus prays that he may dwell within his followers, "I have made your name known to them and will continue to

[127] Buber, p. 85.

make it known, so that the love with which you have loved me may be in them, and so that I may be in them" (John 17:26). He prays that the indwelling that exists between himself and his Father will be reflected both in his relationship with his followers and their relationships with each other, "I have given them the glory you gave to me, that they may be one as we are one. With me in them and you in me, may they be so completely one that the world will realize that it was you who sent me and that I have loved them as much as you loved me" (John 17:22-23).

He predicts that the day will come when they will understand something of the mystery of indwelling, "On that day you will understand that I am in my Father and you in me and I in you" (John 14:20).

In the letters of St. John and St. Paul the mystery of love and indwelling is explored. St. Paul in his letter to the Ephesians prays for Jesus' indwelling with his listeners, "so that Christ may live in your hearts through faith" (Ephesians 3:17). St. Paul offers the classic expression of the Christian's experience of indwelling in his relationship with Jesus, "I live now not with my own life but with the life of Christ who lives in me" (Galatians 2:20).

As the life of Jesus provides you with the example of what human relationships can be, you next may begin to see and express your human relationships in the ways the Scripture writers see and express their relationship with Jesus.

For example, you start with the words of St. Paul, "I live now not with my own life but with the life of Christ who lives in me" (Galatians 2:20). With Jesus as the example of what love is, you can not only make those words of St. Paul your own. You can also expand upon those words and say, "I live, now not I, but those I love and those who love me, live in me." Just as you can say of your relationship with Jesus, "Christ lives in me," you can also say of those you love, "They live in me." Your relationship with Jesus sheds light upon all of your relationships.

St. John says love for one another is the sign of God's indwelling with us: "[A]s long as we love one another God will live in us and his love will be complete in us" (1 John 4:12). As Buber expresses it, "In each Thou we address the eternal Thou."[128] St. John expands indwelling beyond the Christian's relationship with Christ and declares that divine indwelling is to be found in the life of anyone who loves, "God is love and anyone who lives in love lives in God, and God lives in him" (1 John 4:16).

"Following a human relationship to God is like following a river to its sources. If you follow the Amazon to its sources, you come upon many tributaries, and finally you come to a point where you don't know which is the tributary and which is the river."[129] St. Elizabeth Ann Seton writes to her close friend and confidant Antonio Filicchi, "I would cry out now... 'Antonio, Antonio, Antonio'...and my soul cries out: 'Jesus, Jesus, Jesus!' There it finds rest and heavenly peace, and is hushed by that dear sound as my little babe is quieted by my cradle song."[130] One is unable to say where her relationship with Antonio ends and where her relationship with Jesus begins. "You don't know which is the tributary and which is the river."

---

[128] Buber, p. 4.
[129] Buber, p. 6.
[130] Joseph I. Dirvin, *Mrs. Seton* (New York, N.Y.: Farrar, Straus and Co., 1962), p. 161.

Examples of Indwelling

You face a problem in approaching the mystery of indwelling from Scripture examples. The problem is that these verses from Scripture are so familiar in Christian usage that you tend to hear them without listening to them. You tend to look at them without really seeing them. You may be helped by giving the mystery of indwelling more of a human face using the following examples.

Pierre Teilhard de Chardin provides a one-sentence summary of indwelling, "Nothing is precious save what is yourself in others and others in yourself."[131] He then speaks of the death of his sister and the mystery of indwelling:

> Her disappearance has created a sort of universal wilderness around me; it affects every element of an interior world of which I had gradually made her a partner. The two of us thought together in everything that makes up spiritual activity and the interior life. I shall miss her physical presence terribly; on the other hand I think that her power of inspiring and watching over me has strengthened.[132]

In a concentration camp in World War II, Victor Frankl was asked by some of his fellow prisoners to *say* something to them, to help them in their seemingly hopeless situation. We note that underlying his words is a belief in the mystery of indwelling through love:

> I told my comrades...they must not lose hope but should keep their courage in the certainty that the hopelessness of our struggle did not detract from its dignity and its meaning. I said that someone looks down on each of us in difficult hours— a friend, a wife,

[131] Pierre Teilhard de Chardin, *Hymn of the Universe* (New York, N.Y.: Harper and Row, Publishers, 1961), p. 62.
[132] Pierre Teilhard de Chardin, *Letters from a Traveller* (New York, N.Y.: Harper and Row, Publishers, 1957), p. 226.

somebody alive or dead, or a God—and he, she or
they would not expect us to disappoint them. They
would hope to find us suffering proudly—not
miserably—knowing how to die.[133]

Graham Greene's novel *Monsignor Quixote* is an
imaginative expression and story of what might happen if
the original Don Quixote were living at the present time.
The priest from whom the novel gets its title is something
of an oddity. His close friend, Sancho, is the communist
mayor of the town in which he is the parish priest.

The novel is the story of their friendship, including the
death of the priest. After the priest's death Sancho reflects
upon himself and his friend. He reflects upon the mystery
of indwelling through love while not using the explicit
language of indwelling in doing so.

Why is it that the hate of a man...dies with his death,
and yet love, the love which he had begun to feel for
Father Quixote, seemed now to live and grow in spite
of the final separation and the final silence—for how
long, he wondered with a kind of fear, was it possible
for that love of his to continue? And to what end?[134]

In Robert Browning's *The Ring and the Book*, Pompilia,
the wife of Count Guido Franceschini, speaks on her
deathbed of her love for a priest, Canon Giuseppe
Caponsacci, who had attempted to save her life. She
reflects aloud upon the relationships in her life and upon
the words of Jesus, "[A]t the resurrection men and women
do not marry; no, they are like the angels in heaven"
(Matthew 22:30).

In heaven we have the real and true and sure. 'Tis
there they neither marry nor are given in marriage

[133] Viktor Frankl, *Man's Search for Meaning* (New York, N.Y.: Simon and
Schuster, Inc., 1971), p. 132.
[134] Graham Greene, *Monsignor Quixote* (New York, N.Y.: Washington Square
Press, 1982), p. 221.

but are as the angels: right, oh how right that is, how
like Jesus Christ to say that! Marriage-making for the
earth, with gold so much—birth, power, repute so
much, or beauty, youth so much....

Be as the angels rather, who, apart, know themselves
into one, are found at length married, but marry
never, no, nor give in marriage; they are man and wife
at once when the true time is: here we have to
wait."[135]

Jesus' words open up a vision for our imaginations: The
intimacy of the deepest of marriage relationships and of all
love relationships is a sign of and a prelude to an intimacy
that is deeper than that experienced on this earth. Pompilia
sees that in heaven men and women, like the angels, do not
"become married." They are "already married" in the sense
that they possess that deeper union which love at its best
on this earth is pointing toward.

Tennessee Williams' play *The Glass Menagerie*
illustrates indwelling. The narrator, Tom Wingfield, is also
a character in the play. He tells the story of his mother
Amanda, his sister Laura and himself. Each is fragile, as
fragile as the delicate glass figures which are a symbol of
the characters themselves. At the play's conclusion it is
many years later that Tom is reminiscing about those
scenes from his adolescence,

I descended the steps of this fire escape for a last time
and followed, from then on, in my father's footsteps,
attempting to find in motion what was lost in space. I
traveled around a great deal.... I would have stopped,
but I was pursued by something. It always came upon
me unawares, taking me altogether by surprise....
Perhaps I am walking along a street at night.... I pass
the lighted window of a shop where perfume is sold.

[135] Robert Browning, "The Ring and the Book," *The Poems of Robert Browning*, ed. Donald Smalley (Boston, Mass.: Houghton Mifflin Co., 1956), p. 399.

The window is filled with pieces of colored glass, tiny
transparent bottles in delicate colors, like bits of a
shattered rainbow. Then all at once my sister touches
my shoulder. I turn around and look into her eyes.
Oh, Laura, Laura, I tried to leave you behind me, but I
am more faithful than I intended to be![136]

This is an example of the human face of indwelling.
That's what Jesus, St. John and St. Paul are talking about
when they talk about indwelling—the haunting presence of
a loved one. Laura is present with Tom in spite of her
physical absence, persuading him that he is "more faithful
than he intended to be."

Imagining Love Relationships With the Living

You are unable to say what a relationship is. You are
unable to say what love is. You can only say what a
relationship is like and what love is like. When you say
what it is like, you are making use of poetry because the
heart of poetry is imagery in which one thing stands for
another, as when you say, for example, "A love relationship
is like a dance."

Jesus gives us an image of light, "You are the light of
the world" (Matthew 5:14), which can assist us in the
imagining of relationships. We're familiar with concerts or
performances in which the singer or performer is on a
darkened stage, standing under spotlights that illumine the
immediate area where the performer is standing. As the
performer moves from one side of the stage to the other,
the spotlights also move so that the performer is always
walking in a circle of light.

[136] Tennessee Williams, *The Glass Menagerie* in *The Theatre of Tennessee
Williams*, Vol. I (New York, N.Y.: New Directions Books, 1971), pp. 236,
237.

One way you picture your life is that you live your life in the center of a circle filled with light. Like the performer, whether singing or talking or being silent, whether walking back and forth or standing still, you do it within the circle filled with light. All of the spotlights converge upon that circle.

For the performer on stage, at the source of each of those beams of light there is a spotlight creating the light. For you, when you visualize your life as a journey taking place within a circle of light, visualize at the source of each of the beams of light a person with whom you are in relationship.

Anne Morrow Lindbergh helps you to picture a relationship by comparing it to a dance:

> A good relationship has a pattern like a dance and is built on some of the same rules. The partners do not need to hold on tightly because they move confidently in the same pattern, intricate but...swift and free, like a country dance of Mozart's. To touch heavily would be to arrest the pattern and freeze the movement, to check the endlessly changing beauty of its unfolding. There is no place here for the possessive clutch, the clinging arm, the heavy hand; only the barest touch in passing. Now arm in arm, now face to face, now back to back—it does not matter which. Because they know they are partners moving to the same rhythm, creating a pattern together, and being invisibly nourished by it.[137]

To dance is to move within a continuing pattern of coming close and letting go. The "coming close and letting go" refrain in relationships is expanded upon by Rainer Maria Rilke:

> This advance will...change the love-experience which is now full of error, will alter it from the ground up,

[137] Lindbergh, *Gift From the Sea*, p. 104.

re-shape it into a relation that is meant to be of one
human being to another.... And this more human love
(that will fulfill itself, infinitely considerate and gentle,
and kind and clear in binding and releasing) will
resemble that which we are preparing with struggle
and toil, the love that consists in this, that two
solitudes meet, greet, and protect each other.[138]

Imagining Love Relationships With Those Who Have Died

Love relationships include not only the living but also
the dead. John Dunne cites an example from Søren
Kierkegaard to illustrate how the dead remain
contemporary to you:

> The millennia separating me from Abraham, to use
> one of Kierkegaard's examples, are insignificant
> beside the three days it took Abraham to reach the
> top of the mountain where he was to sacrifice Isaac,
> for the millennia are not a time in someone's lifetime
> whereas the three days are such a time and a crucial
> time at that. As a result Abraham and I are
> contemporaries in that no significant lapse of time
> separates us from one another.[139]

The author of the Letter to the Hebrews gives you a
picture with which to imagine your relationship with those
who have died, a picture which enables you to look upon
those who have died as contemporaries of yours. The
writer speaks about heroes of faith, starting with Abraham,
Isaac and Jacob and including many others, "These are all
heroes of faith, but they did not receive what was promised,
since God made provision for us to have something better,
and they were not to reach perfection except with us. With

[138] Rilke, *Letters to a Young Poet*, p. 59.
[139] Dunne, *A Search for God in Time and Memory*, p. 15.

so many witnesses in a great cloud on every side of us, we too, then, should throw off everything that hinders us...." (Hebrews 11:39-40—12:1).

"[S]o many witnesses in a great cloud on every side of us," presents you with a picture. The picture is that at each moment of your life you are sustained and supported in mysterious yet real ways not only by those now living but also by those who have died, those who have preceded you into eternity.

Thomas Merton explains the picture of "so many witnesses in a great cloud on every side of us" in personal terms, "Isaias, Moses, Matthew, Mark, Luke and John are all part of my life. They are always about me.... They are more a part of my world than most of the people actually living in the world. I 'see' them sometimes more really than I see...(those) I live with. I know well the burnt faces of the Prophets and Evangelists."[140]

You can create your own list of "witnesses": all those people who have made a difference in your life, all those who have inspired and do inspire you, be they present or absent, living or deceased. They are your companions.

When you imagine them to be present with you, you are making an unseen reality present and visible to yourself. The reality is that you are connected to those who inspire you, those who love you, those whom you love. Visualizing them as present with you gives you access to the reality of their presence.

Visualizing others with you is a personal, internal process that can be helped by means of other external signs. For example, you keep pictures or mementos of those you love. These pictures or mementos remind you

[140] Thomas Merton, *The Sign of Jonas* (New York, N.Y.: Harcourt Brace Jovanovich, 1979), p. 224.

that when loved ones are absent, they are also present to you. They remind you that loved ones who have died are not only dead but also alive to you.

In a similar way when you enter a church and are in the presence of statues, pictures and icons, these are saying something to you, not only about your connection with God but also your connection with other human beings, past and present.

Your connection with them already exists. What remains for you is to acknowledge the connection. To believe that the connection between yourself and all others exists is to believe in what Christian tradition calls "the communion of saints," namely, a union exists among all the members of the human family, past and present.

Prayer and devotion to the saints rest upon a belief in connections between persons, past and present. When you converse with or pray to a saint or a deceased loved one, or a living loved one who is absent, you are tapping into one of the treasures of the Catholic heritage and, one of the treasures, often unrecognized, of our heritage as human beings. "The growing good of the world is partly dependent on unhistoric acts; and that things are not so ill with you and me as they might have been is half owing to the number who lived faithfully a hidden life and rest in unvisited tombs."[141]

We are indebted to those who have gone before us. I imagine that to reach heaven means to be surprised by at least three things: first, to be there; secondly, to see that we did not walk across the "finish line" but were carried across through the prayer, suffering and love of many known and unknown to us; thirdly, to meet face to face those who

[141] George Eliot, *Middlemarch*, in *The Works of George Eliot* (New York, N.Y.: Nathaniel Moore, 1908), VI, p. 287.

helped bring us through.

I believe this as a consequence of my belief in the resurrection of Jesus. Because I believe Jesus is present in our midst and because I believe that love is stronger than death, I also believe in the presence and influence of those who have died.

The belief that those you love and those who love you live in you is the basis for the belief in our relationship with those who have died as well as with the living. It is the basis of discovering and responding to love relationships not limited by the ordinary notions of time and space. In the words of Marcel Proust, "Souls move in time as bodies move in space."[142] With the help of the writer of Hebrews, you translate this belief into a picture of "witnesses in a great cloud on every side" of you. The picture enables you to visualize the belief expressed by Jesus, "[H]e is God, not of the dead, but of the living; for to him all...are in fact alive" (Luke 20:38).

Questions for Reflection and Discussion

1) What are some examples in your life of the mystery of indwelling?

2) Is it proper to speak of the experience of the absence of God? Give examples.

3) Is it proper to speak of the absence of God? Give examples.

4) Anne Morrow Lindbergh pictures or imagines a relationship by comparing it to a dance. What other ways can you picture or imagine a relationship?

[142] Proust, Vol. III, p. 568.

5) The author of the Letter to the Hebrews uses the image of "so many witnesses in a great cloud on every side of us" to express our connection with heroes of faith who have died. What images or pictures help you to visualize your relationship with deceased loved ones?

6) Thomas Merton gives a partial list of those deceased who are more a part of his world than most of the people living. What are some of the names on your personal list?

Exercise

The thesis of an article by Michael Gallagher (a free-lance writer living in Ridgewood, New Jersey) is that the authority the Church has over you is the people who inspire you.[143]

Make a list of the persons who inspire you, biblical or nonbiblical, living or deceased.

Imagine yourself sitting at the center of a circle. Imagine each of these persons standing at different points on the circumference of that circle.

You look straight ahead and your gaze falls upon a few of them. You look to the left or right and your gaze falls upon others. You don't need to introduce them to each other. They already know each other because of their mutual link with you.

Your response to them will be most of all one of gratitude. You thank them for their presence in your life. You thank them for your awareness of their presence in your life.

You tell them that because of their presence with you, now you know the meaning of the word "gift." Now you

[143] Michael Gallagher, "Divine Inspiration," *Notre Dame*, April 1978.

know the meaning of the word "grace," that unmerited overflow of love that comes to you through them.

Your daily cares, concerns, anxieties, hopes and prayers will be part of your conversation with those who surround you. You also find that your hopes and prayers are not limited to your personal cares and concerns. Your hopes and prayers are becoming global.

In quiet moments you re-create this scene of those who inspire you. As you become accustomed to their presence with you, you find that you can re-create this scene anytime, anywhere. In moments of crisis you will extend the time you spend in their presence.

Suggestions for Further Study, Reflection and Exploration

1) *The Passionate God* (New York, N.Y.: Paulist Press, 1981) by Rosemary Haughton. She develops the theme that we can learn something of the way that God loves people by looking at the way people love people. She concludes that the poetry of passionate love is the accurate language of theology.

2) *I and Thou* (New York, N.Y.: Charles Scribner's Sons, 1958) by Martin Buber.

3) In *The Four Loves* (New York, N.Y.: Harcourt Brace Jovanovich, 1960) C.S. Lewis writes of affection, friendship, erotic love and the love of God. The genius of C.S. Lewis was to write about religious beliefs in general and Christian beliefs in particular in plain English.

Chapter Ten

Stories of Love Relationships

Space and time as we think of them become irrelevant
when we encounter the mystery of love relationships.

Thomas and Therese

A contemporary love story is the story of Thomas and
Therese. Their discovery of each other, or to put it more
precisely, Thomas's discovery of Therese (since she was
already there waiting to be discovered), and the growth of
their relationship once that discovery took place indicate
that their story can be called a love story.

What we know of their relationship comes to us in the
words of Thomas. In the description contained here of their
relationship, phrases and sentences quoted are in his words.

According to his account it was in October of 1941 that
his discovery of Therese took place. She was not unknown
to him prior to that time but only as a casual acquaintance.
She was born and raised in a middle-class family in France.
In the fall of 1941 he was living in America. He
acknowledges in retrospect that he was quite "put off" by
Therese's background, in his words, "the stuffy, overplush,
overdecorated comfortable...mediocrity of the bourgeoisie."[144]

He indicates that although he knew her by sight, it was

[144] Merton, *The Seven Storey Mountain*, pp. 353-355.

a friend, Henri, who introduced him to her and that for the first time he got interested in her—"a fortunate beginning."

It was in October 1941 that Thomas realized the depth of his relationship with Therese: What else would explain such phrases as "the tremendous experience" of discovering her and "ow[ing] her all kind of public apologies and reparation for having ignored her greatness for so long"?

He judges the background from which Therese came quite differently now than the way he did when they were mere acquaintances, "[I]t was an extremely uncharitable judgement of a whole class of people on sweeping, general and rather misty grounds: applying a big theoretical idea to every individual that happens to fall within a certain category!"[145]

"I was immediately and strongly attracted to her—an attraction that...took me, in one jump, clean through a thousand psychological obstacles and repugnances." She has become "a great new friend" and he now sees that "it was inevitable that the friendship should begin to have its influence on my life."[146]

Thomas Merton was born in Prades, France, on January 31, 1915 and died on December 10, 1968. Therese is Therese Martin who was born in Alençon, France on January 2, 1873, entered the Carmelite convent at Lisieux in 1888, died on September 30, 1897, and was canonized a saint in 1925 by Pope Pius XI. The friend who introduced them was Henri Gheon who wrote a biography of Therese.

It is in his autobiography, *The Seven Storey Mountain*, that Thomas Merton speaks of his relationship with Therese of Lisieux:

[145] Merton, p. 354.
[146] Merton, p. 355.

The discovery of a new saint is a tremendous experience.... They become our friends, and they share our friendship and reciprocate it and give us unmistakeable tokens of their love for us by the graces that we receive through them.... And so, now that I had this great new friend in heaven...[t]he first thing that Therese of Lisieux could do for me was to take charge of my brother, whom I put into her care....[147]

Joan, Mark and George

A comparable kind of love story is found in the lives of Mark Twain and George Bernard Shaw in their relationship with St. Joan of Arc. Twain tells the story of Joan through the eyes and words of a fictional narrator; Shaw tells the story of Joan in a play.

Twain insisted that his book on Joan be published with the use of a pseudonym for fear that association with his name would prevent readers from taking it seriously. "I have never done any work before that cost so much thinking and weighing and measuring and planning and cramming, or so much cautious and painstaking execution.... Possibly the book will not sell, but that is nothing—it was written for love."[148]

In a similar vein Shaw claims the direct assistance of the saint in the work he wrote in her honor, "As I wrote," Shaw confided about Joan some years later, "she guided my hand, and the words came tumbling out at such a speed that my pen rushed across the paper and I could barely write fast enough to write them down."[149] Shaw expresses

[147] Merton, *The Seven Storey Mountain*, p. 355.
[148] Mark Twain, *Mark Twain's Letters*, ed. Albert Bigelow Paine (New York, N.Y.: Harper and Brothers, 1917), p. 624.
[149] Shaw, p. xii.

his personal belief in the presence and active influence in one's life of one who has died.

The Bishop and Jean Valjean

Victor Hugo's novel, *Les Miserables*, is a story of sacred moments, the remembering of sacred moments, a story of relationships with the living and those who have died. In other words, it is a love story.

The novel is the story of an exconvict, Jean Valjean, imprisoned for years for the crime of stealing a loaf of bread to help feed his sister and her family. It is a story of the transforming effect that sacred moments can have in one's life. Released from prison, he is rejected by everyone—almost everyone—as an exconvict.

A passer-by suggests he stop at the home adjacent to the nearby church. He is welcomed by Bishop Bienvenu and given a night's lodging. Valjean awakens during the night, decides on a course of action, steals the household's silver plates and runs away. He is caught with the silver and returned to the front door of the bishop's residence under the eye of three gendarmes.

The bishop says to Valjean, "I am glad to see you. But I gave you the candlesticks also, which are silver like the rest and would bring two hundred francs. Why did you not take them along with your plates?"[150]

Valjean is released by the police. In their parting, private conversation the bishop says to him, "Before you go away, here are your candlesticks; take them...never forget that you have promised me to use this silver to become an honest man." Valjean, who had no recollection of any such

---

[150] Hugo, pp. 110-111.

promise, stood confounded."[151]

The bishop continues, "Jean Valjean, my brother; you belong no longer to evil but to good. It is your soul I am buying for you. I withdraw it from dark thoughts and from the spirit of perdition, and I give it to God!"[152]

The remainder of the novel is the story of the remainder of the life of Jean Valjean. It is a story that illustrates that a sacred moment in the life of a human being can have a lifelong effect.

Valjean begins a new life. He changes his name. He works hard. In time he becomes the owner of a factory and amasses considerable wealth. He distributes the wealth with those who work for him and, unknown to anyone, with many who are in need. He is chosen mayor of the town and is beloved by all.

Then his new world is threatened by a crisis. On the night he had stolen the silver plates from the bishop, he had also committed another theft. He now finds out that another man has been accused of being Jean Valjean and accused of that theft.

If he says nothing, the falsely accused man will be convicted and imprisoned. If he reveals his own identity, he himself will be convicted and imprisoned. He sees all of his good works, himself and his soul in the balance, depending on this choice of whether to save an innocent man, "All he had done was nothing, if he did not do that."

He re-lives that moment in his life when he was in the bishop's presence, "He felt that the bishop was there, that the bishop was present all the more now that he was dead, that the bishop was looking fixedly at him.... Men saw his mask but the bishop saw his face. Men saw his life but the

[151] Hugo, p. 111.
[152] Hugo, p. 111.

bishop saw his conscience."[153]

He makes his choice, reveals his identity to the authorities, thereby freeing the innocent man. He is immediately convicted and imprisoned and his conscience is clear.

Sometime later, when he escaped from prison, he took into his care a small orphan girl, eight-year-old Cosette. "This was the second white vision he had seen. The bishop had caused the dawn of virtue on his horizon. Cosette evoked the dawn of love."[154]

Years later, she is engaged to Marius. Valjean has mixed feelings toward Marius who through marriage will deprive him of Cosette. However, in the battle at the barricades during an uprising in Paris, Valjean has the opportunity, unknown to anyone else, to save the life of the unconscious Marius and does so. It is years after the marriage of Cosette and Marius, when Valjean is near death, that Marius finds out who the stranger was who saved him from death at the barricades.

Unaware of the story involved, Cosette describes a package that Valjean keeps near him at all times as "the inseparable." The package contains a pair of silver candlesticks. When he knows he is dying, Jean Valjean lights the candles in the silver candlesticks.

Among his final words in giving the candlesticks to Cosette he says:

> To her I bequeath the two candlesticks which are upon the mantel. They are silver; but to me they are gold, they are diamonds. They change the candles that are put into them into consecrated tapers. I do not know whether he who gave them to me is satisfied with me in heaven. I have done what I could. Love

[153] Hugo, p. 214.
[154] Hugo, p. 392.

each other dearly always. There is scarcely anything
in the world but that: to love one another.[155]

The sacred moments in the life of Valjean were not only
a bridge that touched and extended to all the rest of his life;
they were also a bridge between time and eternity as he
pictures the bishop with him every day of his life but
especially in times of crisis.

Questions for Reflection and Discussion

1) Two candlesticks were a reminder to Jean Valjean of a
turning point in his life which changed everything. What
are some things that serve a similar purpose in your life,
e.g., reminders of a particular period in your life, a
particular person, a particular moment that changed
everything?

2) Who are some of your personal heroes/heroines whose
life stories inspire you?

3) What are some ways in which your heroes'/heroines'
stories have become/can become your own?

4) What are some ways your heroes'/heroines' stories can
influence your life story in the future?

Exercise

Shaw, Twain and Merton each found a person whose life
story was a source of personal inspiration to him.

In the previous exercise you made your personal list of
those who inspire you. In this exercise focus your attention

[155] Hugo, pp. 1199-1200.

upon one of them.

Visualize the person present with you. Keep that mental image of the person before you, tell him/her that he/she has been an inspiration to you. Explain the reasons why you have been inspired. Thank the person for being with you in your life.

Ask for your hero's/heroine's help in a present situation in which you find yourself. Ask "What light can you shed on this matter I'm facing? How would you deal with it?" In this way you are "connecting with" your hero's/heroine's life story in ways that enhance your own story. By imagining the responses of the one who inspires you, you are expanding your own choices. You are deepening and expanding your own life story.

Suggestions for Further Study, Reflection and Exploration

1) Victor Hugo, *Les Miserables* (New York, N.Y.: Penguin Books, 1976). The story of Jean Valjean is now reaching a wider audience through the musical, *Les Miserables* by Alain Boublil and Claude-Michel Schonberg. Lyrics by Herbert Kretzmer. Available in audiocassette from Geffen Records, 9130 Sunset Boulevard, Los Angeles, California 90069.

2) The cover page of Mark Twain's book on Joan of Arc states "*Personal Recollections of Joan of Arc* (New York, New York: Harper and Brothers, 1924) by the Sieur Louis de Conte (her page and secretary), freely translated out of the Ancient French into Modern English from the original unpublished manuscript in the national archives of France by Jean François Alden." The

author's name and the translator's name are both pseudonyms of Mark Twain.

3) *Saint Joan* by George Bernard Shaw (Indianapolis, Ind.: Bobbs Merrill Co., Inc., 1975).

Chapter Eleven

Imagination and Prayer

Does imagination have anything to do with prayer?
Consider the words of Nina to Marsden in Eugene O'Neill's
play *Strange Interlude*:

> The mistake began when God was created in a male
> image. Of course women would see Him that way, but
> men should have been gentlemen enough,
> remembering their mothers, to make God a woman!
> But the God of Gods—the Boss—has always been a
> man. That makes life so perverted and death so
> unnatural. We should have imagined life as created in
> the birth-pain of God the Mother. Then we would
> understand why we, Her children, have inherited
> pain, for we would know that our life's rhythm beats
> from Her great heart, torn with agony of love and
> birth. And we would feel that death meant reunion
> with Her, a passing back into Her substance, blood of
> Her blood again, peace of Her peace!
>
> Now wouldn't that be more logical and satisfying than
> having God a male whose chest thunders with
> egotism and is too hard for tired heads and
> thoroughly comfortless?[156]

Nina wants to expand the understanding of God by
imagining God as Mother. She sees the imagining of God
as Mother as a gateway for bringing qualities of caring and
nurturing into our understanding of God.

So far, so good. However, when she speaks of God as

[156] O'Neill, p. 93.

Father, she reveals an inadequate understanding of her own. For her, God in a male image means, "The Boss...whose chest thunders with egotism...thoroughly comfortless." She has not imagined that God in a male image can be caring and nurturing. She also has not yet imagined that God in a female image may lack these qualities.

It has been said that in the book of Genesis God created human beings in his own image and since then human beings have returned the favor. We tend to "create" or fashion God in our image. This can be beneficial to us as long as we remain aware that images and their meanings and the feelings they elicit fall short of the Mystery we call God that they are attempting to relate to or describe.

The example of Nina illustrates that the images of God we have are images surrounded by feelings. They are images surrounded by our personal experience of "father," "mother," "male," "female." Our images of God reveal much of what our understanding of God is. They also reveal much of what our self-understanding is as well as our understanding of our relationships with others.

Sometimes we come up with wrong answers because we're asking the wrong questions. Nina's words illustrate that the question "Does imagination have anything to do with prayer?" is the wrong question. The question assumes that imagination and prayer are far removed from each other. It assumes that maybe if we try hard enough, we can find some connection between these unrelated subjects.

Nina's words illustrate that imagination has much to do with prayer because imagination is the power through which we picture the God we pray to. So the question becomes, "How can our imagination help us in prayer?"

If we try to conceive of God apart from imagination and

only in terms of "Pure Spirit," such an understanding may seem to exclude the use of imagination in prayer. Whatever we imagine, so the objection goes, is not God. Therefore, so the objection continues, imagination can only "get in the way" of prayer.

Not necessarily so. Granted, what you imagine is not God. However, what you imagine can draw you closer to the Mystery we call God. For example, you sit quietly and imagine yourself surrounded by light. You say to yourself, "The light that surrounds me is God's love." The image together with the specific meaning you give to the image can lead you to a deeper awareness that you are loved by God.

Much of what prayer is for us will depend upon what our self-understanding is, just as our images of God depend to a great extent upon our images of ourselves. Central to Christian self-understanding is the belief that we are the recipients of God's unmerited love—unmerited in the sense that we are loved before we do or intend anything, "[T]his is the love I mean: not our love for God, but God's love for us when he sent his Son to be the sacrifice that takes our sins away" (1 John 4:10).

Unmerited love may also be described as unconditional love. Belief in unmerited or unconditional love tends to go against our grain. We tend to look upon it as "a little too good to be true." If there's one thing human beings find more difficult to accept than bad news, it's good news.

We tend to be suspicious of the story with a happy ending. We tend to be suspicious of the very notion of unconditional love. If we were to believe in unconditional love, what would happen to all of our good deeds and accomplishments that we rely so much upon to assure ourselves that we are lovable? Belief in unconditional love can be called a countercultural belief in our society in which what we do is so often equated with what we are.

For many of us the reaction to being the recipients of unmerited love is, "I cannot imagine being loved like that." Precisely—and that is a part of our problem. We cannot or do not imagine being loved "with no strings attached." Because we don't imagine it, we tend to disbelieve it. In a similar way, if we begin to imagine ourselves as the recipients of unconditional love, we can begin to make belief in unconditional love our own.

To return to the example of imagining yourself surrounded by light, you say to yourself, "The light that surrounds me is God's love. The light reminds me that I am loved by God before I do anything or say anything or attempt anything."

You may be helped in visualizing yourself surrounded by light by the slow repetition of a phrase from Scripture that supports and connects with what you're visualizing, such as, "You are the light of the world" (Matthew 5:14), "[T]he Light has come into the world" (John 3:19), "[Y]ou are all [children] of light" (1 Thessalonians 5:5).

In this way an image from Scripture becomes personal to you because you are connecting it with your life and the way you envision your life. You are making it your own. When you imagine yourself surrounded by light and see that light to be a sign of God's unconditional love, that image together with the specific meaning you give to the image can lead you to a deeper awareness of God's unconditional love for you.

> Sometimes...a wave of light breaks into our darkness and it is as though a voice were saying, "You are accepted," accepted by that which is greater than you and the name of which you do not know. Do not ask for the name now; perhaps you will find it later. Do

not try to do anything now; perhaps later you will do much. Do not seek for anything; do not perform anything; do not intend anything. Simply accept the fact that you are accepted.[157]

When you cultivate this practice of visualizing God's unconditional love as light that surrounds you, something else happens. You carry that image with you so that at any moment or in any circumstance you can be in conscious contact with "the source" within you by picturing yourself surrounded with light.

A Traditional Approach

The use of imagination as a help for prayer is not new. It forms an essential part of the Spiritual Exercises of St. Ignatius of Loyola. In an introduction to his meditations, Ignatius is explicit about the use of imagination as a way of placing oneself in the presence of biblical persons and locations.

> The first prelude is a mental image of the place. It should be noted at this time that when the meditation or contemplation is on a visible object, for example, contemplating Christ Our Lord during His life on earth, the image will consist of seeing with the mind's eye the physical place where the object that we wish to contemplate is present. By the physical place I mean, for instance, a temple or mountain where Jesus or the Blessed Virgin is, depending on the subject of the contemplation.[158]

The Ignatian method is based on the belief that through

---

[157] Paul Tillich, *The New Being* (New York, N.Y.: Charles Scribner's Sons, 1955), quoted in *I'm O.K., You're O.K.* by Thomas Harris (New York, N.Y.: Harper and Row, Publishers, Inc., 1967), p. 237.

[158] Ignatius of Loyola, *The Spiritual Exercises of St. Ignatius,* trans. Anthony Mottola (Garden City, N.Y.: Doubleday and Co., Inc., 1964), p. 54.

your memory and your imagination, you have immediate access to past moments—not only past moments in your own life but also moments in the lives of biblical persons. Just as you have immediate access through memory to past moments in your life, so also you have access through memory to past moments in Jesus' life.

It is not a matter of merely pretending through imagination to be living back in Palestine during the earthly life of Jesus. Rather those moments in his life are accessible to you now in a way similar to the way that moments of your own past life are accessible to you. In each instance the categories of time and space are not barriers. They are overcome by the sympathetic remembering that makes it possible for past moments in his life to be present to you now.

Another Approach

What follows is a kind of reversal of the traditional Ignatian method. This reversal involves a use of imagination but with a difference. Instead of visualizing yourself as present during a scene presented in the Gospel, you visualize the person or persons from the Gospel as present with you on your walk through your life. Instead of visualizing yourself as present, for example, when Jesus is talking to Peter, James and John on the Mount of Olives or in the garden of Gethsemane, you visualize Jesus, Peter, James and John as present with you now in this place where you are.

Instead of imagining yourself as present with Mary and Joseph in Bethlehem or Nazareth, you imagine Mary and Joseph to be present with you as you make your journey this day. Instead of visualizing yourself as a contemporary of biblical persons, you visualize biblical persons as contemporaries of yours.

Prayer becomes not only a conversation between Jesus and yourself but also a conversation between other biblical persons and yourself. Prayer also becomes for you a conversation with nonbiblical persons, for example, personalities in history, those you know and love who have died, and those you know and love who are living. You imagine each of them to be in relationship with you, to dwell with you as you walk through your life. Prayer is a way we remain in contact with those we love. Therefore prayer is not only a conversation between yourself and God. It is also a conversation between yourself and those you love.

The Mass: An Imaginative Approach

The close union between past moments and the present moment can be seen by reflecting upon the Mass's meaning. The Mass involves remembering. In the Liturgy of the Word we remember what Jesus said. In the Liturgy of the Eucharist we remember who he was and what he did. We follow and repeat and remember what he did at the Last Supper, "This is my body...do this in memory of me.... This...is...my blood..." (Luke 22:19-20).

While the Mass is a remembering, it is more than a remembering. We believe in the real presence of the one we are remembering. Thus we speak of the Mass as a living memorial in which in some mysterious way the past and the present are joined through his real presence among us.

The presence of Jesus is not limited to the Eucharist.

His presence in the Eucharist casts light upon his presence in any and all of life's moments and situations.

Pierre Teilhard de Chardin sheds light upon the mystery of death and resurrection in the life of Jesus and in our own lives through imagery, the imagery of the bread and wine at Mass. He makes connections between bread and wine and the Mass on the one hand and our own personal experience on the other.

First he distinguishes between our activities and our passivities. Activities are everything we do and accomplish, all of our labors. Passivities are everything that happens to us, everything that enters our life. Our passivities are of two kinds: the passivities of growth and the passivities of diminishment. Passivities of growth are everything good that enters our life, everything that strengthens, supports and sustains us. Foremost among these passivities of growth is life itself, which is received by us and given to us far more than we imagine. The passivities of diminishment are all the evils of life: the disappointments, the heartaches, the separation, the dying, everything which in any way diminishes or lessens our life.

Next Teilhard de Chardin describes our activities, as well as the passivities of growth, as the bread of our life. By way of contrast all the evils of life—the passivities of diminishment—may be described as the wine of our life. At times the bread of our life tends to dominate our thoughts and feelings. These are the times when we feel that it's good to be alive; life is beautiful and we appreciate ourselves and others as well.

At other times the wine of our life may tend to dominate our thoughts and feelings. These are the times when we feel that life is a burden, when nothing goes right and no one seems able to help. At times one and at times the other may tend to be foremost in our life, but each day there is bread and there is wine, the joys and the disappointments, the hopes and the heartaches.

With all of this as a starting point we turn to our vocation of discovering and responding to the presence of Jesus in different ways. We respond to the presence of Jesus under elements of bread and wine by our belief in this mystery of faith, "This is my body.... This is my blood." However, our discovery of the presence of Jesus does not end there. It only begins there as a starting point to discovering his presence elsewhere.

When we look to the lives of other people, we see the bread and wine of the lives of others. In striving to respond to others' bread and wine, we fulfill St. Paul's words, "Rejoice with those who rejoice and be sad with those in sorrow" (Romans 12:15).

Hence, to believe in the Mass means not only to believe that Jesus continues to speak his words over bread and wine; it also means to believe that over the bread and wine of our own life, over the bread and wine of others' lives, over the bread and wine of the entire human family, Jesus continues to speak his words, "This is my body.... This is my blood."

Teilhard de Chardin speaks of human development in relation to the Mass, "It seems to me that in a sense the true substance to be consecrated each day is the world's development during that day—the bread symbolizing appropriately what creation succeeds in producing, the wine (blood) what creation causes to be lost in exhaustion and suffering in the course of its effort."[159]

In "Mass on the World" Teilhard de Chardin writes:

Receive, O Lord, this all-embracing host which your

[159] Teilhard de Chardin, *Letters from a Traveller*, p. 86.

whole creation, moved by your magnetism, offers you at this dawn of a new day.

This bread, our toil, is of itself, I know, but an immense fragmentation; this wine, our pain, is no more, I know, than a draught that dissolves. Yet in the very depths of this formless mass you have implanted— and this I am sure of, for I sense it—a desire, irresistible, hallowing, which makes us cry out, believer and unbeliever alike: "Lord, make us *one*."[160]

Teilhard de Chardin summarizes his thought with a prayer:

Do you now therefore,...pronounce over this earthly travail your twofold efficacious word: the word without which all that our wisdom and our experience have built up must totter and crumble—the word through which all our most far-reaching speculations and our encounter with the universe are come together into a unity. Over every living thing which is to spring up, to grow, to flower, to ripen during this day say again the words: This is my Body. And over every death-force which waits in readiness to corrode, to wither, to cut down, speak again your commanding words which express the supreme mystery of faith: This is my Blood.[161]

Perhaps in the end it all comes down to this: We don't just attend Mass. Rather our life *is* a Mass. Bread. Wine. Body. Blood. Being offered. Being spent. Being poured out. "Lord, grant that we may see."

[160] Teilhard de Chardin, *Hymn of the Universe*, p. 20.
[161] Teilhard de Chardin, *Hymn of the Universe*, p. 23.

Questions for Reflection and Discussion

1) Is your God male or female or both? Give examples.

2) What are some examples in which your imagining of God has changed from one period of your life to another?

3) What are some examples from your experience of human beings fashioning God in their own image?

4) What are some examples in which "creating" God in a human image is helpful?

5) What are some examples in which "creating" God in a human image is harmful?

6) What are some examples to illustrate that at times if there's one thing human beings find more difficult to accept than bad news, it's good news?

7) Which approach to prayer is easier for you: to imagine yourself as present with Mary and Joseph in Bethlehem or to imagine Mary and Joseph to be present with you as you make your journey this day?

8) What are some examples from your experience of prayer as a conversation between you and those you love?

Exercise

This exercise is an expansion of the reversal of the traditional Ignatian method. Instead of visualizing yourself present with biblical persons in their biblical setting, you visualize biblical persons with you in your personal setting.

Choose the biblical persons to whom you feel the

closest. Visualize the particular biblical person. Welcome the person into your presence. Thank the person for being here. As, for example, Thomas Merton confided his brother to the care of St. Therese, you may want to place some person, some situation, some aspect of your life under the protection of the biblical person you have chosen.

At times you will visualize the biblical person unaccompanied by words of your own. At other times your words and/or prayers may help. When you are visualizing the presence of a biblical figure with you, what you are imagining to be happening, is happening.

Suggestions for Further Study, Reflection and Exploration

1) *The Spiritual Exercises of St. Ignatius Loyola* (Boston, Mass.: The Daughters of St. Paul, 1978) makes explicit use of imagination in visualizing biblical persons and biblical events.

2) *Mysticism: A Study in the Nature and Development of Spiritual Consciousness* by Evelyn Underhill (New York, N.Y.: E.P. Dutton, 1961). Using the traditional distinctions of the purgative way, the illuminative way and the unitive way, Underhill explores the history of mysticism in the West.

3) *Sadhana: A Way to God: Christian Exercises in Eastern Form* by Anthony de Mello (Garden City, N.Y.: Doubleday and Co., Inc., 1984). *Sadhana* is an Indian word meaning discipline, technique, spiritual exercise, approach to God. The book has four major headings,

"Awareness," "Awareness and Contemplation,"
"Fantasy" and "Devotion."

Chapter Twelve

Another Name for Love

Robert Browning gives us an imaginative expression of the final moments of St. John the Evangelist's life in a poem entitled "A Death in the Desert."

John reflects aloud upon his own life story as the last of those who saw and heard what Jesus said and did. A few of his disciples are with him.

> ...it is long
> Since James and Peter had release by death,
> And I am only he, your brother John,
> Who saw and heard, and could remember all....
> If I live yet, it is for good, more love
> Through me to men: be nought but ashes here
> That keep awhile my semblance, who was John—
> Still, when they scatter, there is left on earth
> No one alive who knew (consider this!)
> —Saw with his eyes and handled with his hands
> That which was from the first, the Word of Life.
> How will it be when none more saith, "I saw"?[162]

John sees his writing summarized in the thought that human beings "should, for love's sake, in love's strength believe."[163] He sees life's questions come down to one question:

> Does God love,

---

[162] Robert Browning, "A Death in the Desert," *The Poems and Plays of Robert Browning* (New York, N.Y.: Random House, Inc., 1934), p. 297.
[163] Browning, "A Death in the Desert," p. 297.

And will ye hold that truth against the world?[164]

He speaks of the pain of absence from his Lord. Yet whatever Love wishes is now his sole desire,

> For if there be a further woe....
> Wherein my brothers struggling need a hand,
> So long as any pulse is left in mine
> May I be absent even longer yet,
> Plucking the blind ones back from the abyss,
> Though I should tarry a new hundred years![165]

His self-surrender has reached a point that he prays that he may endure the pain of absence from his Lord yet longer if he can thereby "lend a hand" to any of his brothers and sisters. This attitude of the evangelist parallels the story that is told of Buddha who instead of taking the step toward "final enlightenment" chooses instead to return to the circle of the human family and to share the enlightenment he has already received.

Evelyn Underhill cites Richard of St. Victor's description of "the steep stairway of love" by which the contemplative ascends to union with the Absolute. The stage in which the soul is utterly concentrated on the one, is not the final stage. It is the next to final stage.

The final stage is the one in which the person

> accepts the pain and duties in the place of the raptures of love; and becomes a source, a "parent" of fresh spiritual life. The "Spouse of God" develops into the "Mother of Divine Grace." That imperative need of life to push on, to create, to spread, is here seen operating in the spiritual sphere. This forms that rare and final stage in the evolution of the great mystics, in which they return to the world they forsook; and there live, as it were, as centers of transcendental energy, the creators of spiritual families, the partners

---

[164] Browning, "A Death in the Desert," p. 297.
[165] Browning, "A Death in the Desert," p. 308.

and fellow-labourers with the Divine Life.[166]

Robert Doran notes, "Mystics of various traditions speak of a state of detachment from inner states and outer objects, where detachment is not unrelatedness but free, nondemanding relatedness."[167] And Martin Buber writes:

> What does it help my soul that it can be withdrawn anew from this world here into unity, when this world itself has of necessity no part in the unity—what does all 'enjoyment of God' profit a life that is rent in two? If that abundantly rich heavenly moment has nothing to do with my poor earthly moment— what then has it to do with me, who have still to live, in all seriousness still to live, on earth? Thus are the masters to be understood who have renounced the raptures of ecstatic "union."[168]

Nathaniel Hawthorne's novel *The Scarlet Letter* concludes with a description of "the remainder" of Hester Prynne's life:

> ...[A]s Hester Prynne had no selfish ends, nor lived in any measure for her own profit and enjoyment, people brought all their sorrows and perplexities and besought her counsel, as one who had herself gone through a mighty trouble. Women, more especially— in the continually recurring trials of wounded, wasted, wronged, misplaced, or erring and sinful passion—or with the dreary burden of a heart unyielded, because unvalued and unsought—came to Hester's cottage, demanding why they were so wretched, and what the remedy! Hester comforted and counselled them, as best she might. She assured them, too, of her firm belief, that, at some brighter period, when the world should have grown ripe for it, in Heaven's own time, a new truth would be revealed, in order to establish the whole relation between man and woman on a surer

---

[166] Underhill, *Mysticism*, p. 140.
[167] Doran, Article III, p. 860.
[168] Buber, p. 87.

ground of mutual happiness.[169]

In Charles Dickens' novel *A Tale of Two Cities* Sydney Carton confides to Lucie Manette, "For you and for any dear to you, I would do anything.... Think now and then that there is a man who would give his life to keep a life you love beside you."[170]

Years after Lucie's marriage to Charles Darnay, Darnay is arrested and condemned to death during the French Revolution. Sydney Carton makes arrangements for Lucie, her father and daughter to leave France for the safety of England. Then Carton who bears a striking resemblance to Darnay manages to restore Darnay to his family. He smuggles Darnay out of the prison by taking his place in the prison cell.

On the night before Carton's execution,

> They said of him, about the city that night that it was the peacefullest man's face ever beheld there.... If he had been given an utterance to his,...they would have been these:
>
> "...I see the lives for which I lay down my life, peaceful, useful, prosperous and happy, in that England I shall see no more....
>
> "I see that I hold a sanctuary in their hearts.... I see her and her husband, their course done, lying side by side in their last earthly bed, and I know that each was not more honoured and held sacred in the other's soul than I was in the souls of both....
>
> "It is a far, far better thing that I do, than I have ever done; it is a far, far better rest that I go to than I have ever known."[171]

[169] Nathaniel Hawthorne, *The Scarlet Letter* (New York, N.Y.: Holt, Rinehart and Winston, Inc., 1963), p. 253.

[170] Charles Dickens, *A Tale of Two Cities* (New York, N.Y.: Dell Publishing Co., Inc., 1976), p. 198.

[171] Dickens, pp. 478-480.

In James Joyce's novel *Ulysses* Molly Bloom is reflecting upon the relationship between Lucie Darnay and Sydney Carton. The reflection takes place as part of a "stream of consciousness" by Molly expressed by the unpunctuated sentences:

> it must be real love if a man gives up his life for her that way for nothing I suppose there are few men like that left its hard to believe in it though unless it really happened to me... to find two people like that nowadays full up of each other that would feel the same way as you do.[172]

Near the end of her life St. Therese of Lisieux wrote,

> I feel that my mission is to begin—to make others love God as I love Him...to teach souls my little way.... I will spend my heaven doing good upon earth.... No, there cannot be any rest for me till the end of the world—till the angel will have said, "Time is no more."[173]

The ceremony called beatification is one of the steps toward the Catholic Church's declaration of an individual as a canonized saint. Edith Stein was beatified by Pope John Paul II in Cologne, Germany, on May 1, 1987.

She was a German Carmelite nun of Jewish descent who died in the Holocaust at Auschwitz. Her name in the Carmelite Order was Sister Teresa Benedict of the Cross.

Each Carmelite nun composes a final Testament. In 1939 Edith Stein wrote hers:

> May the Lord accept my life and death for the honor and glory of his name, for the needs of his holy Church...for the Jewish people...for the deliverance of Germany and peace throughout the world and finally, for all...living and dead whom God has given me: may

---

[172] James Joyce, *Ulysses* (New York, N.Y.: Random House, Inc., 1976), p. 767.
[173] Therese of Lisieux, *Autobiography of Saint Therese of Lisieux* (New York, N.Y.: P.J. Kenedy and Sons, 1926), p. 231.

none of them be lost.[174]

At Auschwitz in 1941 a prisoner has been condemned to death by starvation:

> Suddenly another prisoner, breaking ranks, asks to take the condemned man's place. Even the SS are stunned. Having reduced the personal identities of twenty thousand Poles to numbers, for once they want to know more about a victim.
>
> "Who are you?" one SS man asks number 16,670.
>
> "A Catholic priest," the prisoner replies. "I have no family," he adds, as though that explains everything. An undercurrent runs through the camp: "It's Father Kolbe." Even those who are not his friends recognize the name—the famous Franciscan, the editor, publisher, and opinion-molder whose publications were so influential in prewar Poland.
>
> What is he thinking of? Even the Bible of his faith says only, "Greater love than this has no man—that he lay down his life for a friend." The doomed man is not even a friend of Kolbe's.
>
> "Well, you see," one of Kolbe's intimates interjects, "for Father Kolbe everyone is a friend."[175]

John Dunne writes,

> Seeing with God's eyes...is not seeing something other than you see with your own, but realizing or recognizing what you are seeing, realizing your connection, recognizing your kinship with what you are seeing, saying (as God does in Scripture), "I know you." Feeling with God's heart, if Love gives us the eyes, is not feeling something other than you feel with your own, but being willing to feel what you are feeling, being willing to have the connection or the kinship, saying (again as God says in Scripture),

[174] Waltraud Herbstrith, *Edith Stein: A Biography* (San Francisco: Harper and Row, Publishers, 1985), p. 95.

[175] Patricia Treece, *A Man for Others* (New York, N.Y.: Harper and Row, Publishers, 1982), pp. vii-viii.

"I am with you."

When I am heart and soul, mind and strength in
loving God, I am sharing in humanity, finding human
wholeness in relation to God. When I am seeing
human suffering and feeling the inhumanity of one
human being to another, on the other hand, I am
sharing in divinity, seeing with God's eyes and feeling
with God's heart. I can see in the image of the
suffering Christ how sharing in humanity, entering
heart and soul into human existence, leads to sharing
in divinity, to becoming vulnerable with God's own
vulnerability to human injustice and human
suffering.[176]

In Shakespeare's play *The Tempest* Prospero possesses
divine powers. His invisible messenger who fulfills his
commands is a spirit by the name of Ariel. Those who
harmed Prospero earlier in his life are now in his control.
Then Prospero goes one step further—a step beyond
justice, in a conversation with Ariel.

Ariel speaks about Prospero's enemies:

> "Your charm so strongly works 'em
> That if you now beheld them your affections
> Would become tender."

Prospero asks, "Dost thou think so, spirit?" Ariel
replies, "Mine would, sir, were I human." Prospero replies,

> And mine shall.
> Hast thou, which art but air, a touch, a feeling
> Of their afflictions, and shall not myself,
> One of their kind, that relish all as sharply
> Passion as they, be kindlier moved than thou art?
> Though with their high wrongs I am struck to th' quick,
> Yet with my nobler reason 'gainst my fury
> Do I take part. The rarer action is
> In virtue than in vengeance. They being penitent,

[176] John S. Dunne, *The Church of the Poor Devil* (Notre Dame, Ind.: University
of Notre Dame Press, 1983), pp. 141, 154-155.

> The sole drift of my purpose doth extend
> Not a frown further. Go release them, Ariel.
> My charms I'll break, their senses I'll restore,
> And they shall be themselves.[177]

Prospero gives up his control of those who have harmed him. He releases them from his power. He lets them be themselves rather than be subject to his control. He forgives them. Then he renounces once and for all his divine powers. He becomes a human being again.

The desire of Prospero to become fully human is a reflection of the desire of God to become fully human. It is a reflection of the emptying of God in the person of Jesus of whom St. Paul speaks:

> His state was divine,
> yet he did not cling
> to his equality with God
> but emptied himself
> to assume the condition of a slave,
> and became as men are;
> and being as all men are,
> he was humbler yet,
> even to accepting death,
> death on a cross. (Philippians 2:6-8)

Another name for love is compassion.

Questions for Reflection and Discussion

1) What are some examples of Robert Doran's description of detachment as free, nondemanding relatedness?

2) Using John Dunne's distinction of sharing in humanity and sharing in divinity, what are some examples from your experience of your sharing in humanity?

[177] Shakespeare, *The Tempest*, V, i, 17-32.

3) What are some examples from your experience of your sharing in divinity?

4) What are some examples from your life, using Molly Bloom's words, of something that's hard to believe in unless it happened to you—that has happened to you?

Exercise

This is an exercise, in John Dunne's words, of "seeing with God's eyes" and "feeling with God's heart."

Here you become more aware of what you've already been doing. You visualize a person with whom you are connected through prayer. You surround this person with light that is God's love. Your action is to imagine the light being intensified around that person. While you watch that light being intensified, you say, "I love you."

You are now doing what God is doing—loving. In loving another, you are aware that loving God is not "an extra step" or "something added" to what you're now doing. Loving God *is* what you are now doing. You are "recognizing what you are seeing, realizing your connection" by saying "I love you." You are loving another human being and you are loving God. You are sharing in humanity.

It doesn't stop there. Sharing in humanity leads into the next stage—sharing in divinity. Loving another through prayer, praying for another, surrounding the other with the light of God's love not only affects that person. It also affects you.

Your prayer for and with the other, your connection with the other enables you to say, "I am with you in what you're going through." You give your "Yes" to that connection, "being willing to feel what you are feeling, being willing to have the connection." Now you are sharing in divinity, "becoming vulnerable with God's own vulnerability to human injustice and human suffering."

You now know from personal experience that there is a "conspiracy" at work in this world above and beyond *all* the human conspiracies of harm and hate. This conspiracy is love and this conspiracy is what you are called to. The conspiracy of love continues and deepens.

Suggestions for Further Study, Reflection and Exploration

1) *Franny and Zooey* (Boston, Mass.: Little, Brown and Co., 1962) by J.D. Salinger. Franny is recovering from a kind of nervous breakdown. She is very much into the recitation of "the Jesus prayer." With the help of her brother, Zooey, Franny learns that Jesus is to be found not only in prayer but also in other members of the human family.

2) *A Man for All Seasons* (New York, N.Y.: Random House, Inc., 1962). Robert Bolt's play of the life of St. Thomas More is the story of a man who sees his life as finally not a matter of reason but a matter of love.

3) *Edith Stein, Philosopher and Mystic* (Collegeville, Minn.: The Liturgical Press, 1990) by Sister Josephine Koeppel, O.C.D., is a biography of Edith Stein, a woman for all seasons.

Credits

Material from *A Man for Others* by Patricia Treece, copyright ©1982 Patricia Treece, published by Our Sunday Visitor in arrangement with Harper & Row, Publishers, is used by permission.

Material from *Answer to Job* by Carl G. Jung, trans. R.F.C. Hull, copyright ©1954 by Bollingen Foundation, Inc., is reprinted by permission.

Material from *A Testament of Hope: The Essential Writings of Martin Luther King, Jr.*, edited by J.M. Washington, copyright ©1986 by Coretta Scott King, Executrix of the Estate of Martin Luther King, Jr., is reprinted by permission.

Material from *Autobiography of Saint Therese of Lisieux* by Therese of Lisieux, copyright ©1926, published by P.J. Kenedy, is used by permission of Macmillan Publishing Co.

Material from *Book of the Month Club News*, Summer 1987, page 5, is reprinted by permission of the publisher.

Material from *Brideshead Revisited* by Evelyn Waugh, copyright ©1945 by Evelyn Waugh, published by Little, Brown and Co., is used by permission of the publisher.

Material from *Brideshead Revisited* by Evelyn Waugh, copyright ©1945 by Evelyn Waugh, published by Little, Brown and Co., is used in Canada by permission of Sterling Lord Literistic, Inc.

Material from *Christ and Prometheus: A New Image of the Secular* by William F. Lynch, S.J., copyright ©1970 by University of Notre Dame Press, is reprinted by permission of the publisher.

Material from *Christianity and Evolution* by Pierre Teilhard de Chardin, copyright ©1969 by Editions du Seuil, English translation copyright ©1971 by William Collins Sons and Company, Ltd., London, is reprinted by permission of Harcourt Brace Jovanovich, Inc.

Material from works by John Dunne: *The Church of the Poor Devil*, copyright ©1982 by John S. Dunne; *A Search for God in Time and Memory*, copyright ©1967, 1969 by John S. Dunne, C.S.C.; *The Way of All the Earth*, copyright ©1972 by John S. Dunne, C.S.C., is reprinted by permission of the publisher, Macmillan Publishing Co., a division of Macmillan, Inc.

Material from *The Complete Stories* by Flannery O'Connor, copyright ©1971 by the Estate of Mary Flannery O'Connor, is reprinted by permission of the publisher, Farrar, Straus and Giroux, Inc.

Material from *The Confessions of St. Augustine*, by St. Augustine, trans. John K. Ryan, copyright ©1960; *Notes on How to Live in the World...and Still Be